Necessary
Conversations

Necessary Conversations

Between adult children and their aging parents

*Suggestions for discussing finances,
medical care, driving, and living
arrangements — before the crises hit.*

Gerald W. Kaufman and L. Marlene Kaufman

Good Books

Intercourse, PA 17534
800/762-7171
www.GoodBooks.com

Design by Cliff Snyder

Cover photograph © Bloomimage/Corbis

NECESSARY CONVERSATIONS
Copyright ©2013 by Good Books, Intercourse, PA 17534
International Standard Book Number: 978-1-56148-798-1
Library of Congress Catalog Card Number: 2013937633

Publisher's Cataloging-in-Publication Data
Kaufman, Gerald W.
    Necessary conversations -- between adult children and their aging parents / by
Gerald W. Kaufman and L. Marlene Kaufman.
    p. cm.
    ISBN 978-1-56148-798-1
1. Adult children of aging parents. 2. Adult children of aging parents --Family
relationships. 3. Aging parents --Care. 4. Aging. 5. Parent-child relationships. I.
Kaufman, L. Marlene - II. Title.

HQ1063.6 K38 2013
646.7/8 --dc23   2013937633

Table of Contents

This book is dedicated to all of you who have shared so richly with us from your family stories. We learned much from the partnerships you have created. Thanks for letting us listen in on your conversations.

Preface

The idea for this book came from a seminar that we presented with our daughter Anne and her husband, Todd. We had been asked to talk about the conversations parents and their adult children need to have about aging. At the time of the seminar, we were in our late sixties, and Anne and Todd were in their early forties. As we gathered material for the seminar, it became clear that this was a timely subject for many people. The seminar was well attended, and the responses from it revealed an intense interest in the subject.

Besides the seminar, the book is also drawn from our nearly forty years as counselors. Many of the families with whom we worked faced significant conflict with parents in their senior years. Few had made plans or had even talked together about the future. When crises arose, the families were unprepared.

Writing this book has been very rewarding. When friends and colleagues learned what we were doing, many offered stories from their own lives, or they referred us to others with experiences to share. There are many more stories waiting to be told; they can be a part of the ongoing conversation.

As we gathered these stories, we visited many people in their homes. We appreciated their openness and warmth. It was especially gratifying to experience their spirit of humility and wish to make sure all of their family members were given the credit they deserve. Some allowed us to use their names, while, for a variety of reasons, others did not. However, every story is real in the important details. We are indebted to those who were a part of this process.

The community in which we have lived for more than three decades, Lancaster County, Pennsylvania, has also shaped our ideas. A blend of urban and rural areas with more than half a million residents, it sits on the western edge of the East Coast megalopolis, about a ninety-minute drive from Philadelphia and Baltimore.

Perhaps the most important influence in our lives is the Mennonite community of which we are members. We belong to a more progressive branch of the Mennonite church, but we are surrounded by many Amish and Old Order Mennonites, who demonstrate the importance of family ties and simple living. Our views are shaped by these relationships. Many of the stories in the book are from people who are part of these communities, but we have listened to and included a diversity of voices, all of which have strengthened our understanding of the relationship between parents and their adult children.

When to begin these conversations?

We suggest that the retirement of parents is a convenient marker for the parent-adult child conversations about aging to begin. For most families, that means the parents will be in their sixties, and their adult children will be in midlife.

This will take effort. Adult children may live far away and be very busy with their own lives. Since many families get together during holidays or for other occasions, we propose that you use some of that time to discuss your shared future.

For readers who have no children, we suggest that you petition a niece, nephew, or some trusted younger person to play the role of coach and supporter. If you are deep into your retirement years, we encourage you to begin this relationship soon. We believe that the conversations which we describe in the book can be useful to everyone regardless of their situation.

We also recommend that every congregation or house of worship designate someone to provide counsel and support to its aging members—especially those with no adult children. For readers who have no faith community, we suggest that you seek counsel from friends and professionals who work with seniors. No person or couple should age alone.

It is our strong belief that families need to begin these discussions early and continue talking until the death of their parents. Far too many families wait until circumstances force them to talk, and then they have to make decisions under pressure, which often leads to conflict that can continue for years.

We encourage families to find new ways to connect with each other. Many families have disconnected from each other emotionally. This powerful shift in the culture has exacted a high toll on families. We believe that there are better ways to face the later years of our lives. That's what this conversation is all about.

It is our hope that this book can help families work together to make important decisions about aging. We hope it will encourage adult children to support their parents throughout their senior years.

One note: We have written most of this book in the voice of the parents. The exception is chapter 4, which we have written in the voice of the adult children.

To all the people at Good Books, a big thanks for believing in this project. We are especially grateful to Phyllis, Merle, and Kate for their advice, editing, and optimism. They helped to give shape to ideas that need to be a part of the conversations as we age.

And now we give thanks to our adult children — Brent and his wife, Cheryl; Nate and his wife, Cathy: Anne and her husband, Todd; and Nina and her husband, Craig, for joining us in our process of aging. Your support, advice, and courage to help us face ourselves and our future have enabled us to better understand what this partnership is all about. Let's keep the conversations going.

— Gerald W. Kaufman and L. Marlene Kaufman

CHAPTER 1

Beginning the Conversations

MOM: *You know, last night when we went out to dinner and they asked if we wanted the senior discount, I just about said no. Really, were you ready for that? Seniors! We're not old yet. Why do they have to rush the calendar? I want to stay young as long as I can.*

DAD: *Taking a senior discount doesn't make you old. We're only old if we think we are. Besides, who doesn't want discounts these days. We can get better rates at hotels, concerts, and lots of other places. Look, we don't have to even think of being old for another twenty years, so don't lose any sleep over some little discount.*

DAUGHTER: *Mom called today and was upset because they were offered a senior discount at a restaurant last night. She was embarrassed—maybe even offended. She's not ready to think about being old. Now every time they go out, she says aging stares them in the face. Are they going to be confronted with this discount thing? I tried to tell her how young she looks and how everybody their age goes through the same thing, but I don't think she's convinced.*

SON: *I'll call Mom and get her straightened out. There's no need for her to be so upset about such a small thing. Mom and Dad shouldn't be so uptight about their age. I don't know what their plans are for the future, but at their age, it isn't a big deal now. They should be happy for the discounts. Besides, you and I have plenty of our own things to worry about.*

As we approach our senior years, many of us don't think much about what is ahead. Often we are in good health and active, and our lives are going well. So our thoughts center on cruises, golf, hobbies, and, perhaps most of all, the freedom to do nothing. When a what-if thought crosses our minds, we quickly push it aside, telling ourselves that we'll deal with it when the time comes.

Thinking about the future, though, is important to do now. And beyond thinking, we need to talk, first with our spouse and then with our adult children. Like it or not, we are all in this process as families together. Even if we have talked with our spouse about what is ahead, many of us have not done so with our adult children. Some surveys indicate that only about one-third of parents have talked with their children about aging, and often not until a crisis occurs.[1] Some medical crises may make it impossible for us to convey our wishes to the family.

That's one reason it is important to begin these conversations with our adult children around the time of our retirement, when most of us as parents are still well and competent. If we have made it to our sixty-fifth birthday, statistics indicate that at least seventy percent of us will live at least until we are eighty-five.[2] The possibility that we could live for twenty or more years makes it even more important to have formed an open relationship with our adult children.

Among many other things, we should be sure to talk about our finances, our health, where we might want to live as we continue to age, and how we want to be cared for when our health declines. It is especially important to talk together about end-of-life decisions. Most of all, we want these conversations to be ongoing ones because our needs will change as we age.

Living in a complex world

We invite our adult children to become involved with us because we live in a world that is becoming too complex to handle by ourselves. This complexity is a special challenge for us when, according to brain scientists, our ability to process information begins to slow down. We can become more susceptible to making wrong decisions. Seniors are often the victims of scams. It can also be hard for us to know how to respond to legitimate appeals for money from various charities or church organizations and those that come even from our adult children.

The fact that our society now presents us with many more choices than in previous generations adds to that complexity. In his book *The Paradox of Choice,* Barry Swartz notes that choice making has become an enormous burden for all Americans, taking up precious time and using up our energy. For seniors, one of the many choices we have to make is in selecting the right Medicare supplement plan from the dozens of confusing options that are available. We often need help with the ever-changing technology that confronts us daily, including knowing how to use computers, TV remotes, digital cameras, and even our cell phones with all their apps. It is with some embarrassment that we ask our grandchildren how to make them work.

Our resistance to asking for help

There are many reasons, though, that we don't initiate these conversations with our adult children. We don't want to burden them during a very demanding time in their own lives. They are often feeling pressure from their careers and from raising their families. For the most part, we aren't on their minds, and we want to keep it that way.

In addition, many of us were influenced by parenting theories that emphasized the importance of not placing too many demands on children. Author Lori Gottlieb says that parents were encouraged to give their children the freedom to find themselves and the encouragement to do anything they wanted in life. Now, when we need them, it may be hard to change that pattern. After all, they are now their own persons, and we don't want to be co-dependent on each other. Or so goes the theory.

On the other hand, according to an AARP study, seventy percent of our adult children are still receiving some financial support from us.[3] So when they are dependent on us in this way, can we expect them to become our partners during a time of need?

In fact, many of us have a strong aversion to becoming dependent on anybody. Throughout our adult lives, we have prided ourselves on being self-sufficient. Most of us had careers that were significant and satisfying. We were active in our church and in the community. We made most of our decisions by ourselves. So as we enter this phase of our lives, it is hard to shift gears. In the backs of our minds, the word "dependency" is accompanied by the words "decline," "disability," "dementia," and "death." These things are too unpleasant to think about, so we put off the discussion with our adult children for another time.

Readiness

Whatever our situation, our adult children need to be old enough, and mature enough when we invite them into this conversation. Starting too early can create problems. Marion and Verna found that out when—in their fifties—they attempted to prepare their son and daughter—then in their twenties—for what would happen if Marion and Verna died suddenly. The urgency to start this discussion was driven by the fact that both had lost their mothers at a young age. They didn't want their children to be unprepared for this situation. However, the children were not ready to face that idea, so they postponed the discussion until the children were older and ready. The next time it went well.

There are other reasons, though, that some families have trouble talking about aging. For some it is mainly because the parents have had a negative relationship with their children for most of their lives and now can't break out of the pattern. Other families don't talk about aging because they have difficulty talking about anything. The discussions can also be hard if there is conflict among the children. Too many of us put the discussions off because we are procrastinators and don't want to face what is coming.

Lack of models

Sometimes we find it hard to talk with our adult children because we had parents who didn't talk openly about their lives. Maybe they thought that we didn't have a right to know anything about them. Perhaps they wanted to be in control and couldn't give up the power of the parent's role. Some didn't want to open up because it would have meant revealing unpleasant things about their pasts, like hidden debts, risky investments, or even moral failures.

But the most likely reason that our parents didn't talk with us was that they had no models for doing so. Most of their parents died at a younger age, and there simply wasn't time or a need to plan together for their future. In addition, our grandparents often had a sense of fatalism. Many believed that the future was in God's hands, and thus, they should "give no thought to the morrow." They saw no point in planning for the future. But now that most of us are living deep into our senior years, it is time to create a new model and to plan for the future with our adult children.

Facing an unwelcome life stage

Planning for our future isn't something we look forward to because, for the first time in our lives, we are entering a life stage that we *don't* want to be in. Few people—if any—actually want to get old.

That is very much in contrast to our earlier life stages. As toddlers, we wanted to walk. In fact, our parents said we ran before we walked. Later, we were excited about starting school. When we became adolescents, we couldn't wait to drive. After graduating from high school, many of us eagerly anticipated going to college, starting careers, getting married, having children, buying homes, and traveling.

Now, instead of being in a stage of growth, we are entering a stage of decline—what is sometimes called *entropy*. Instead of gains, we begin to think more about losses. We think about the past more than the future.

We have images of wrinkled bodies, failing memories, and loss of significance. Instead of beginnings, we think of endings. Because these are unpleasant thoughts, we tend to keep them to ourselves.

Society's influences

These thoughts can be pushed off more easily because we are surrounded by a culture that is obsessed with staying young. The messages that come to us imply that delaying aging is an option. We see images in the media of seniors who are enjoying vibrant lives. They are dancing the night away, rafting on white water, and sitting in bathtubs by the ocean. Advertisements encourage us to take medications to correct every age-related infirmity. None of the models used in those ads are hunched over or on wheelchairs. Cosmetic surgeons promise to take away our wrinkles and reshape our bodies. The messages suggest that changing the outside will also change the inside. These voices of denial in the culture even shape the language we use. No one is old; we are just "senior citizens," and the time we are living in is always "golden." Euphemisms have a way of numbing us to the many realities that are a part of aging—at least for a time.

In some ways we are still young

On the other hand, there is some truth to the fact that we *are* younger than our parents were at this age. For many of us, seventy is the new sixty. Generally, we are healthier, and we think and act younger than our parents did. Instead of being incapacitated seventy-year-olds who are housebound, many of us are traveling the world and engaging in activities that we didn't have time for earlier. We take up new hobbies or expand old ones. We audit courses at local colleges, and many of us find new meaning through volunteering.

Some of us are kept more youthful by staying active with our grandchildren. Increasingly, we engage in exercise programs that keep our bodies and minds sharp. More of us are enjoying our work so much that we put off our retirement; others choose new careers or work part-time. All of these activities have a profound effect on how we age and make it easier to convince ourselves that we will never get old.

This sense of immortality has been aided by advances in medical care. Instead of being invalids due to damaged knees or hips, we can remain mobile by having joint replacements. Many of us have gotten another lease on life after heart surgery. We have medications that help control blood pressure, diabetes, and cholesterol. Our lives are extended through various cancer treatments. So not only are we living longer, our quality of life is better. In some ways we really *are* younger.

With this sense of invulnerability, some of us are choosing a lifestyle that helps us believe we will be around for a long time. We build large homes to accommodate our many possessions, create significant estates, travel the world, and make long-term plans that suggest that nothing will change. We are a part of a powerful generation that made enormous changes in our world. We put a man on the moon and believed that nothing could stop us from going to Mars. The new frontier was ours to explore and to conquer. Aging couldn't possibly get in our way.

To our surprise, we may find our net worth declining because of changes in the economy. Our world seems somehow less secure. Optimism is being replaced by doubt. We might have to take a loss when we try to sell our property, or we discover that our investments aren't what they once were. Some of us still carry significant debt and recognize that we might have to take a few steps down from our previous lifestyle. In order to survive financially, some of us may even need to work longer than we planned.

Aging in place

One of the most important questions that confronts us is whether we can remain in our homes when we get older. In response to the growth in the population of seniors, the aging-in-place concept has significantly expanded, so that in-home nursing care, rehabilitation, hot meals, transportation, and emergency call buttons are available. All of this may require modifications to our homes so that we are able to remain where we are for a longer time. This option is much less expensive than being cared for in nursing care facilities.

In Sarasota, Florida, the oldest large county in the United States, approximately one-third of the population is over sixty-five.[4] Planners in that community are seizing on the presence of this demographic to develop new programs to care for seniors in noninstitutional settings. A coordinating agency of seniors and professionals within the SCOPE program there works to improve services to seniors and to use the skills of those who are still high functioning.

One of their initiatives, Institute for the Ages, supports research that will provide new ideas for other communities to apply to their populations. A seminar hosted by the institute included a presentation by Eric Dishman, Director of Health Innovations at the INTEL Architecture Group. His company is creating technologies that will detect early physical and mental changes in seniors through the use of a smart carpet and electronic ankle bracelets. Dishman believes that early detection, followed by physical changes in the home, can prevent falls. Technologies being tested by other companies can monitor whether medications are being taken properly. These companies believe that technology will enable seniors to live healthier and more productive lives while remaining in their homes.

Learning from the past and other cultures

Aging in place is not a new concept. Several generations ago, adult children typically took in older parents. When I (Marlene) was a young child, my seventy-year-old grandfather came to live with my family after his second wife died. My parents and we nine siblings warmly welcomed him. He brought humor with his storytelling and was a positive influence on our family. He was never an intrusion and was an active part of the family life. I have good memories of him helping to peel peaches and watching him trim the grapevines. He died at our home at age eighty-four. My mother was his primary caregiver.

That pattern is present in various ethnic communities in North America and around the world. While serving as relief workers in Vietnam, Mark and his family observed the interaction of three-generation families in their courtyards. From the balcony, he often saw grandparents sitting among their grandchildren as they played. The parents were working as professionals in the city.

Don and Anna Ruth Jacobs, who spent more than twenty years as missionaries in Africa, found seniors being cared for—and valued—within the family in what are called *mji* in Swahili, or "family villages." Lawrence Chiles, a bishop in the Koinonia Fellowship of Churches, also observed that in African families he visited, there is a great deal of respect shown for the elderly. He says the Swahili term to describe the relationship children have with the elderly is *shikamoo,* meaning "I grasp your feet." The response of the elder, though, is *mara- haba*—"Don't overdo it." Children bow low when they greet their elders as a sign of respect.

In the African American community in the United States, Lawrence says the church plays an important role in setting the tone for relationships among generations. Many congregations have a "mother of the church," who serves as a disciplinarian for the children and even as an unofficial advisor to the pastor. Three-generation households are common. It is expected that elderly parents will be cared for within the home of one of their children.

Lawrence's wife, Nereida, grew up in an Hispanic home where her mother cared for her elderly mother for eleven years, and later for her father. When Nereida thought about her own future, she worried that she would become a burden on her children. However, when Lawrence and Nereida told their three adult children that they were considering moving to a continuing-care community in the future, the children all responded, "Don't even give it a thought. We will take care of you when that time comes!" Their response came as a pleasant surprise. The children also expressed concern about their parents' adjustment to retirement.

Tony described how prevalent three-generation households were when he was growing up in Puerto Rico. His sister cared for their parents in her home until they died. Although that pattern is changing somewhat in the Hispanic community in the United States, Tony's four children have made it clear to him and their mother, Dorothy, that they will be welcomed in their homes at the point that they need care.

Within the Amish and more conservative Mennonite groups, it is assumed that adult children will care for their parents. Parents rarely go to nursing homes. Often a small house is built nearby on the property of one of the children. The Amish build a small apartment, called a *grossdawdy* house, onto the main house. In some situations, parents spend time in each of the adult children's homes to reduce the responsibility on any one family. Sometimes the care of parents is shared among the siblings.

As we gathered with John and Mary in their simple Amish home, the sun was setting. For a while we "English" visitors strained to see our hosts across the room and wanted to reach for a light switch. But our hosts were able to adjust to natural changes in the light. Darkness was not something that needed to be driven out, or so it seemed. When the right time came, they produced their kerosene lamps and turned them on. The lights flickered and hissed but didn't give off the same brightness that we have come to expect in our light-biased world. To John and Mary, light, dark, and the shades in between were a natural part of their daily lives. We had come to their home to learn more about how Amish families live together in a *grossdawdy* house. If we wanted to see one firsthand, we had come to the wrong place. The zoning board had denied John and Mary's request to add an apartment onto their home. So we visited with them in the new house that they built just up the hill from their original home, where their son and his family now live.

Even though they aren't living in the same house, they are close enough to allow daily contact with their son's family. Several other adult children and their families are just a short carriage-ride away. John and Mary are clearly a part of a family village. John helps his son on the farm, and Mary and the women of the family work together to preserve food from their gardens. John and Mary have a large room in the basement to accommodate their children and grandchildren for meals.

Within this "village," Amish values of simple living and separation from the surrounding culture encourage families to stay connected through the life cycles, making it possible for them to reject Social Security and Medicare and care for aging parents in their own homes. John and Mary emphasize that almost no older Amish members live in nursing care facilities. Adult children take turns attending to parents, even those who have dementia. Children who live far away take their turns caring for aged parents, often staying a week or more.

As John and Mary anticipate the future, they do so with the assurance that the Amish culture has prepared a way for them. Just as they accept the darkness of night, they also accept the naturalness of aging and dying. They experienced that close up when they gave care to their parents. Now they take comfort knowing that care will be provided for them.

Realities in the parent-adult child experience

In mainstream American culture, we frequently encounter challenges in forming family partnerships that meet the needs of parents as they age. Because many of us will live into our mid-eighties and beyond, it is more important than ever that we talk about our shared futures. To form meaningful partnerships with our adult children, we have to address the following challenges:

- *We have fewer children*

    In the past, large families allowed for the possibility of three-generation households. Today the average family is much smaller. Obviously, that reduces our choices and can place a heavy responsibility on those fewer adult children. And some of us have no children.

- *We had children when we were older*

    We married later than our parents did and were older when we had our children. Our children are likely to be in early adulthood when we retire. They may just be starting families and careers and may not be ready to assume responsibility for us.

- *Our children may live in other communities*

    For several generations, adult children have scattered to different parts of North America and the world to pursue careers and other opportunities. It is less likely that they will live in our community. This not only reduces our emotional connection with them, it also means that we can't count on as much support from them.

- *We now live much longer*
  Because many of us can expect to live about twenty or more years after retirement, our adult children may need to be concerned about us for a much longer time. Although we can receive some support from community agencies, someone needs to serve as the coordinator to assure that our needs are being met. Generally our adult children do that best.

- *Many of us are divorced*
  Increasingly, seniors are divorced when they begin retirement. They may also have adult children who are divorced. Divorce can cause mixed loyalties, remarriages, and other issues. This disruption in family life can be overwhelming when it comes to planning for our senior years. Above all, it can cloud the parent-adult child relationship at the very time we need to be forming a new partnership with them.

Between our conversations

Purposeful conversations between parents and adult children can be challenging, but they are important. Family meetings can help everyone develop common goals and create a plan that guides decision-making. Here are suggestions about how to get the conversations started:

- Parents can take the lead in setting up the meetings.

- Parents can explain why the partnership is important and how it might work.

- Adult children can express their feelings about this new relationship, ask questions, talk about what they can offer, and reveal their areas of interest and skills.

- Discussions should include finances, housing needs, health, and end-of-life wishes.

- It is helpful if someone takes minutes and then distributes copies to the parents and children.

- To accommodate adult children who live at a distance, try to schedule meetings on holidays or during vacations. Conference calls and Skype can also be helpful.

- The goal is to develop a plan that conveys the wishes and needs of the parents and their adult children. The plan should be updated as circumstances change.

Ending thoughts

As we enter our senior years, a partnership with our adult children helps us plan for the future. Failing to have these conversations can lead to decision-making in a crisis and to undesirable outcomes. Aging goes better when the people who are most directly involved have worked together to create a plan based on carefully considered choices. Let the partnerships begin!

Questions for parents

1. What would keep you from forming a partnership with your adult children?

2. Without this partnership, what is your plan to meet your needs during your senior years?

3. Should we just hope that everything will work out on its own?

4. How can your adult children be the most helpful to you?

CHAPTER 2

The Conversation Within

DAD (TO SELF): *Last month the boss looked so happy at his retirement party. He talked about the traveling he and his wife were finally going to do. About how nice it would be when he could get tee time during the week when the golf courses aren't so crowded. But when I saw him at church a month later, he admitted that he missed work—the socializing, the structure, and even the respect he felt when he was CEO. I was surprised that he talked that openly.*

I'm only a couple of years away from retirement. I've tried not to let work be my whole life, but I'm not big on hobbies. And I can't see myself pushing wheelchairs around the hospital. I know some men enjoy volunteering, but somehow it seems like busy work to me—something people do to keep from getting bored. After years of having a job that has been very satisfying, maybe I'll have the same experience as my boss when I retire. It might be best if I just keep working.

MOM (TO SELF): *After 30 years of teaching I'm ready for something else. The district has a good plan for teachers who retire early. I don't need the job. And every year the kids are harder to teach. It seems that half of my students are on medication for ADD. Parents aren't as supportive as they used to be. Now they just take the side of their child and blame the problems on teachers.*

Besides, our daughter could use some help with her children now that she has gone back to work. I felt bad when I couldn't help her before when she really needed it. It will also be easier for me to visit Mom in the retirement community. She keeps calling me. I feel guilty when I can't go to see her as often as she wants.

We all carry on conversations with ourselves. Self-talk began when we were young children. We carried on animated discussions with imaginary playmates. During our teen years, some of us used diaries for this purpose. Adults don't speak with imaginary playmates, and most of us don't write in diaries, but we still talk with ourselves. In fact, self-talk is a vital way to process what is going on around us and within us.

We tend to guard our inner conversations intensely. When we were very young, we stopped the chats with our imaginary friends when someone came into the room. We kept the secrets private during our teen years by locking or hiding our diaries. Now when we are asked what is on our minds, we get uncomfortable and often give general answers. As when we were younger, we still prefer keeping our inner thoughts to ourselves.

Concealing thoughts about aging

The wish to conceal private thoughts may even increase as we enter our later years. We may try to ignore these thoughts by jumping headlong into new activities, travel, and frenzy. But for each of us life is changing and the future is uncertain. Like it or not, our identity is being redefined, and our life purpose is in flux. We have much to ponder but little that we are ready to share with other people.

In part, we keep our thoughts—especially negative ones—to ourselves because we don't want to worry others or make them think they have to solve our problems. Mostly, though, we hide these thoughts because we are protecting a side of ourselves that we aren't ready to have others see. That side contains our fears, self-doubts, and disappointments. We do, after all, have an image to maintain, and showing our insecurities may reveal something that we want to keep to ourselves. We may even keep these thoughts from those closest to us, especially our spouse and adult children.

The emotional part of our inner conversation may be the hardest to talk about. How do we explain feeling less valued by a loss of status since retirement? We aren't included in important meetings, the phone no longer rings, and incoming emails have all but disappeared. We wonder why friends from work no longer call us to go out to lunch. At the same time, we discover that lifting the bag of salt for the water softener is more of a challenge, and opening jar lids is harder. Ultimately, we are thinking about being in the last stage of life, which can be hard to talk about.

If we do talk with our adult children, it is usually about less emotional subjects—our 401(k), friends, trips we want to take, and maybe moving to a smaller house. These situations are rather straightforward and objective.

Sometimes we talk because we have to. An offer to sell a house or a decision about buying a car might motivate us to talk with our adult children.

Inner thoughts of adult children

While we ponder the future, our adult children likely have their private thoughts about us. In the early part of our senior years, they won't feel the same kind of concern that we do, especially if we are still working and in good health. However, thoughts about our futures probably aren't far from their minds, especially as we retire—a marker they can't ignore. They, too, may wonder how we will adjust, whether we will want to spend more time with them, what our financial situation is, whether we might move from the homeplace, and how our marriage will handle the change.

When they are more reflective, they might wonder what their lives will be like when our health declines or when one of us dies. Their lives are already busy enough with their own families. The term, sandwich generation, begins to take on real meaning when they let their minds go a bit. If they have few siblings—or none—or live at some distance from us, they are beginning to realize that the coming years will be more complex and challenging for them, especially if they need to care for us.

So they usually also withhold their inner conversations, because they aren't sure how we would respond if we knew what they were thinking. And they keep their thoughts to themselves because the thoughts may be unpleasant. Indeed, it may take a crisis—like a sudden illness or a financial problem—to get the conversation started. But even then, their words may be measured and tentative.

Anticipating retirement

In the years leading up to retirement, we often think positively about what lies ahead. We look forward to the freedom of no longer carrying as much responsibility. We anticipate being our own bosses and determining how we spend our time.

We hear about the ways we can contribute to society and dream of the good things that can happen when we retire. We look forward to spending more time with grandchildren. Some of us create a to-do list of unfinished projects. We promise ourselves that we will work on getting our bodies in shape. Others of us dream about buying an RV for a long trip across the country.

What if?

Scenarios slip into our minds. What if we don't have enough money and need to delay retirement? What if we get bored? What if we miss our friends at work? What if we get on our spouse's nerves?

Although we try to push these thoughts out of our minds, we still wonder how our lives will change if we have a heart attack or develop a disabling illness. These thoughts are made more real if we are having trouble climbing steps or losing some of our coordination. However, we usually don't entertain these thoughts very long. We are on a countdown to freedom.

Life after the retirement party

We turn in our keys and clean off our desks. We close the book on a lifetime of work. Then the moment arrives for our retirement party with gifts and speeches. Coworkers talk about how much they'll miss us and promise to stay in touch. There are tears as well as laughter.

What helped to define us throughout our adult years has now disappeared. We are now a former teacher, a former nurse, a former business owner, a former salesperson. When we meet people, we can no longer say who we are by what we do. We think about how awkward our conversations will be. Learning a new social language may not be easy for us. We wonder who we are now if we aren't doing something significant.

Rethinking identity

For a while after retirement, our inner conversations center on who we are now becoming. We were identified very closely with our careers. They opened doors, gave us a kind of respect, and carried with them a kind of pedigree. What we did was who we were. Now it is difficult for us to think of ourselves in any other way.

This new identity crisis evolves slowly for some of us, and for others not at all. Although men tend to connect their identities to their work more than women do, that too is changing now that more women have developed long and satisfying careers outside the home. We are aware that we need to find something that will bring us new meaning and new identities. But at the beginning of retirement, it is hard to imagine.

New freedom

Initially we enjoy the new freedom. We sleep in. We don't care—or even remember—what day of the week it is. Our work uniforms remain unused in the closet and are replaced by everyday clothes. We play golf or tennis when we want to. The headaches that we brought home from work are now gone. Our inner conversations are filled with dreams for what we can finally do. Breakfast at restaurants with our retired friends becomes a regular event, and we look forward to the next time we will be together. It fills an empty space for us.

What now?

But after the last sip of coffee, we return to a house that now seems strangely empty. It used to be the refuge to which we returned after long hours of work. It was a special place to recover from the wounds of battle. Now it is silent and somehow less welcoming. In the midst of our new freedom, we have a feeling that something is missing.

But the house hasn't changed at all; it isn't really empty. Maybe the emptiness is within us. The void can't completely be filled by golf and breakfasts with friends. Yes, the trip to Hawaii was wonderful, but the memories wore off quickly. We know we can't find contentment just through traveling. We may even tire of the projects that we have set up for ourselves or find them difficult to complete. We had been eager to get started on them, but now we wonder why we have lost interest in finishing them. Maybe it's because we've made too many birdhouses or knitted more afghans than we have use for.

We become aware that what needs to emerge is a person who finds new ways of relating and giving to others. While this new person is an extension of the former one, the emerging one will have a more realistic understanding of what is now possible and important. Replacing the earlier busyness with a new busyness will not bring the comfort and contentment we are seeking. The only thing that will bring that is finding new meaning and an acceptance of *being* more than *doing*. But that idea works better in theory than it does in reality. We wonder how we can just *be* without doing something. Meditating doesn't come easily for some of us.

Physical changes

Our bodies are showing signs of aging. Every day, it seems, we sag a little more. We've given up trying to shed the extra pounds. Our hair is thinner, and we may stop trying to hide the gray. We begin to notice that we are less steady on our feet and have trouble reaching our toes to cut our nails. It's a challenge to hear conversations in a noisy room. At class reunions, we feel discouraged when old friends aren't quite sure who we are. If at one time we felt attractive, we feel less so now. Having others tell us that we have a pleasing personality may be well intentioned, but it somehow feels patronizing. And we feel somewhat irritated when people tell us "how good you look for your age."

It worries us that we take daily medications to control cholesterol and blood pressure. Pillboxes are for old people. We experience more pain and find it a challenge to play competitive sports. We tire more quickly. It's common to nod off in the evenings while reading or watching TV.

Most of the time we convince ourselves that these things are mere annoyances. It could be worse. When we are with our friends, our common laments help create a spirit of camaraderie. Increasingly we share inner thoughts as we compare health-status reports. We attempt to rub salve on our emotional wounds with humor. For now, though, we try not to complain because much of life is going well. For the most part, our thoughts of uncertainty remain within.

Dependency and death

We remember news of our peers who died unexpectedly or were diagnosed with life-threatening illnesses. If we had a serious illness, would any of our friends want to hear about it or even care? We have known for some time now that our college roommate is in a nursing home with ALS. Now when attending funerals, we think we see fear in the eyes of our peers. For the first time in our lives, we can't escape the images of disability and even death. We think more about end-of-life issues. Perhaps most of all, we fear becoming dependent on others. Being self-reliant is deeply ingrained in how we see ourselves.

We briefly consider what it would be like if our spouse died. We imagine enormous feelings of emptiness and grief. Could we survive financially? Could we cope day to day? It is hard to think of remarrying because of loyalty to our spouse. What would it mean to our children and grandchildren if one of us died? We don't want to dwell too long on that reality.

Search for peace

But that all seems far away in our early retirement years. When we think clearly, we know the numbers are on our side. Our parents lived well into their eighties, and the doctor tells us we're in good shape. We push our worst-case scenarios off for another time. We must seize the day. There is much to live for.

We begin to feel comfortable being around our spouse more. We were worried about getting on each other's nerves, but we are adjusting to the changes retirement has brought in our relationship, and that feels good. Developing new skills in cooking, doing the laundry, or checking the air pressure in the car tires has actually been liberating. We enjoy new activities and have found meaningful volunteer assignments in the community. We're reassured.

We feel lucky that we are in a community where lots of cultural programs are available. Senior discounts help. Our church has a monthly gathering for senior members. We're finding a new life. We're becoming somebody different than we were. It's not so bad. In some ways it's better because we're not tied down with expectations. We're not competing. Maybe we're discovering what just *being* means. We know that it's better than *not* being.

Spiritual awakenings

Many of us think more about spiritual things. While we had times in the past when we felt close to God and belonged to a supportive congregation, ultimate meaning was diluted by immediate reality. Generally, little that happened in our lives led us to deepen our spirituality. We were too busy and maybe too self-satisfied.

Now more aware of the fading sun, we form a new interest in what lies beyond. We may be more comfortable sharing our thoughts and fears.

Ending thoughts

It's probably good that we don't say everything that's on our minds. But we can be too private and miss out on the benefit of other people's wisdom, as well as their support, when we don't share our important thoughts. Because we are in a new life stage that includes decline and endings, we're likely thinking about whole new areas. We may have self-doubt and uncertainty about our emerging identities.

Often we worry about what is coming. Unfortunately, many of us carry these thoughts alone. But we need to speak openly to others who love us and can give us some perspective. Mostly that sharing can lead to problem-solving and to the creation of a plan that can help us face our future with more clarity. When we keep these thoughts to ourselves, we tend either to minimize their importance or let our imaginations get the best of us. Talking is something we must do with our spouses, adult children, friends, pastors, doctors, and sometimes, with counselors. Now more than ever, we must share our inner conversations so that we can face this new life more clearly.

Learning to reveal private thoughts

- Keep a journal.

- Have daily breakfast conversations with your spouse about private thoughts.

- Schedule monthly klatches with a trusted friend.

- Express concerns and hopes to adult children on your birthday.

- Take some action to face your biggest concern and, if possible, resolve it.

Questions

1. What is your biggest worry when you think about your future?

2. If you haven't shared that worry with anyone, why not?

3. What gives you purpose now?

4. Is just *being* enough for you?

CHAPTER 3

Marital Conversations

WIFE: *I'm starting to worry about how much you're just sitting around watching TV—especially sports. You keep saying that you deserve a break, but it's been a few months now. You know the yard needs mowing, and our son could use some help with the deck he's building. And I'm bothered by your grumpiness. I thought we were both looking forward to retirement. We had lots of dreams. It has to be better than this.*

HUSBAND: *I still can't figure out where you get all your energy. You're running all over the place, from committees at church to always being over at our daughter's. I thought when we retired we'd take it easy. Maybe you're right about the TV. I know the yard needs to be mowed, and I'll call our son to see if he needs help. But it's hard not to have any schedule now. Before, every day of my life was planned. Now every day is a big blank. I still can't figure out why it all seems so easy for you.*

After years of looking forward to retirement, we have both finally arrived. Freedom from the demands of work feels good to both of us. Our loyalties are no longer divided. Our marriage doesn't have to take second place to work. Our focus can now be on each other. The phone doesn't ring with requests to come in to work early or to make one more trip for the company. Neither of us has a distracted look as we sit across the breakfast table from each other. Perhaps the greatest gift is that we don't have to set the alarm clock for another day filled with responsibilities. And we anticipate more time with our grandchildren.

We have been planning a long time for a post-retirement trip to celebrate this milestone. But now it is behind us. We saw some wonderful scenery and had lots of uninterrupted time to talk. It gave us an opportunity to learn to know each other in a new way. Returning home and establishing a new routine also feels good. We have to admit that living out of a suitcase and having no schedule was getting old.

These celebratory trips can bring out differences between us, and the lack of focus can create stress for which we aren't prepared. Partway into their trip, Daryl and Lila wished they had made better decisions about it. Daryl was eager to start the trip because he had been retired for several years and was biding his time until Lila retired. They sold their home, purchased a motor home, and planned a trip with flexible destinations and few deadlines. They soon found themselves directionless and in tension with each other. Lila missed the satisfaction from her work and her friends and felt displaced by not having a home to return to. Daryl, however, was enjoying the adventure and the freedom of not having deadlines and schedules.

In the midst of their frustrations came a welcome discovery at an art gallery they visited. Lila realized she would like to develop a framing business that would complement her work as an artist. Daryl supported the idea and drove back to the art gallery to learn more about the framing business. During the rest of the trip, they spent many good hours planning for the new business. Soon after they arrived home, they bought a house that could be adapted for Lila's new studio. That discovery has been important to both of them in the years since then.

No preparation

When we enter retirement, many of us aren't prepared to face the changes to our marriages—especially having more unstructured time together. Although we may have tried to prepare by seeking advice about finances, housing, and Medicare supplements, few of us thought about how retirement could affect our marriages. In fact, the glossy brochures that we received in the mail showing couples who are smiling, embracing, or engaging in invigorating activities made it look so easy. Nowhere did we hear about the adjustments that we would both need to make. What we didn't get was an orientation to retirement.

Ironically, we were given orientations to virtually every change that came along throughout our lives, beginning with kindergarten and continuing through the time we enrolled in college. We received trainings for our jobs, premarital counseling, birthing classes, tours of the birthing center, and classes to prepare us for parenting. Now, in a highly challenging transition in our lives, we are left to make this adjustment on our own.

More years together

Maybe the concept of needing an orientation to retirement hasn't been a priority because retirement itself is relatively new. Several generations ago, people didn't live nearly as long, and so, comparatively few retired. In the early 1900s, my (Marlene's) maternal grandmother died at the age of twenty-eight, and my paternal grandfather died when he was twenty-three. The first broadscale recognition of retirement in the United States didn't take place until 1935, when the Social Security program was created.[1] For the first time, persons who lived to age sixty-five could count on receiving a pension and could retire. Longevity has increased since then, and most of us expect to have many more years after retirement. Fiftieth wedding anniversary celebrations are now commonplace.

While this opportunity to be together for additional years is a wonderful gift for many of us, it is not without its challenges. For example, it is typical to experience a vacuum in our lives when we leave our jobs. This lack of structure can cause spouses to get on each other's nerves and experience conflict in ways that didn't happen when one or both were working outside the home. Typically, men more than women feel a lack of purpose and a loss of self-worth. Often women find more meaningful things to do. These differences can take spouses by surprise.

We are also continuing to figure out our roles in the midst of a cultural shift that has taken place in the last several decades. In our parents' generation, gender roles were much more distinctly defined. Men did "men's work" and women did "women's work." Now many roles are shared and the lines are blurred. Those changes become even more pronounced after retirement, especially if one of us insists on maintaining traditional roles. If we work at adjusting to these changes and are open to talking about these differences, our relationship can be strengthened.

Another cultural shift concerns our increased expectations of high levels of marital performance. The media has flooded us with advice about achieving personality compatibility, improving sexual techniques and better communication skills, and resolving conflicts. Couples are led to believe that to have a good marriage, they must be soul mates. During retirement those expectations can be magnified. We can no longer escape scrutiny by running off to work.

Many of us know couples—some of them our friends—who apparently failed the test and divorced. Unrealistic expectations become a part of our marriages in the years before our retirement and follow us even now. Spouses who are more realistic and don't see their relationship as a performance to be evaluated can live with imperfections—and happily! But many of us never stop rating our spouse.

Ordinary time together

Fortunately for most of us, what *brought* us together is still what *keeps* us together. Even though the physical attraction is different now than when we first met, the positive characteristics we saw in each other are still there—humor, warmth, compassion, energy, and stability. Some of us have been strengthened by our shared faith. Life experiences have deepened our relationship—the sickness of children, the deaths of friends, financial challenges, and successes.

What may have strengthened us most were the ordinary moments—the cuddling, back rubs, the sharing of chores, taking turns getting up with a sick child at night, long trips to visit the children in college, and the many times when nothing in particular was happening. As in the past, most of the time our conversations are still ordinary—about the weather, what to have for dinner, the grandchildren, events at church, and who is winning the most money on *Jeopardy*. These chats are the foundation of marriage at all ages—nothing profound—but they keep us informed and connected. Now in retirement, we depend on the ordinary moments even more than in the past. We accept every day as a gift and know that we can't take each other for granted. At this point in our lives, intimacy takes on a new meaning.

Settling unresolved differences

During this time, we ought to face and resolve unsettled issues between us while we are still able to do so. It is a time to reflect openly on the painful times and seek healing and forgiveness for past hurts. Over the years we may have acted in ways that were hurtful. In a variety of ways we may have been unfaithful to our vows. It is important that we find a way to seek and grant each other forgiveness. We shouldn't wait for another day, because that day may never come. Too many marriages have ended at the sudden death of a spouse before the couple could forgive and reconcile. The grief of these survivors can never be resolved.

To help avoid living with regrets, Peter and Elfrieda Dyck made a commitment early in their marriage to practice forgiveness daily. Before going to sleep, they would utter the phrase *nichts zwischen uns* in their native German language, meaning, "There are no unresolved differences between us," as they went to sleep. They kept that promise throughout more than fifty years of marriage. When Elfrieda died, Peter had a sense of peace, knowing that nothing was left unresolved.

It is also vital that we work out our differences for the sake of our adult children. Jim and Sue recognized that there were some ongoing issues between them, and they sought marriage counseling. As a part of their healing, they invited their adult children to a weekend gathering at a retreat center. There they asked forgiveness for the impact that their conflict had on the children during their growing-up years. The children were touched by their openness and granted forgiveness. They shared tears of joy. The whole family celebrated together in a new way. This set the stage for having Jim and Sue's adult children join them as partners in planning for the many changes that were to come as their parents began to decline.

Shared responsibilities

In our pre-retirement years, many of us developed rather distinctive marital roles that were often shaped by career demands, schedules, and by our preferences and abilities. For the sake of efficiency, the responsibilities that we accepted tended to follow a predictable pattern: wives did the cooking, husbands did the yard work. In retirement we realize that the tasks we did before may need to change—in part because of fairness and in part because of necessity. We may even go through a period of uncertainty about the changes. Until we make those changes, tasks may not be done efficiently, and our relationship may suffer.

Many of us negotiate our way through these changes. Willingness to learn new skills strengthens our relationship and prepares us for the declining health or death of a spouse. It is important for both of us to learn all life skills needed for daily living. If we hadn't developed those skills before, we need to begin learning them the day we retire.

Conversations about free time

In the early years of retirement, many of us have trouble knowing how to spend our free time. Some of us put energy into neglected work around the house. We clean out any spare rooms and spaces and get rid of things that we no longer need. But when those tasks are finished, many of us don't know what to do next. When there are no particular schedules or demands, we can lose focus. Our motivation sags, and we can sink into apathy. Others of us find it difficult to get started on projects or to complete those we began. We may find ourselves getting into pointless arguments.

We who have part-time work or serve as volunteers can be invigorated by these opportunities. Many of us develop hobbies or take up some form of recreation. While we do many of these activities individually, we can find it very satisfying to do new things together, such as gardening, cooking, playing tennis, or volunteering as a team.

One of the most important ways we can find meaning at this time is by expanding the time we spend with friends. Although they were important to us before, we need them now more than ever. They are a valuable source of love and support and can bring a freshness that spouses need to keep them from becoming stale with each other.

Conversations about health and caregiving

One of the most urgent conversations to have together at this time is about our health. Many of us avoid talking about it because we are in good health. Others of us avoid the subject because we aren't ready to face our eventual decline—and death. It is common to ignore health changes in ourselves and our spouses long after others see them. The change may be as minor as a hearing loss. It may be more life threatening, like being unable to walk up a flight of steps without pausing several times.

It is important to talk with each other about our health because some illnesses can be resolved or minimized by early treatment. Even when the illness cannot be cured, it is important to discuss how we want to approach that reality. Neglect usually makes the condition worse. Unfortunately, it is common for couples to put off talking about health until they are forced to. Then when one spouse is incapacitated from a stroke, dementia, or is in a coma from an accident, the other spouse is left to make decisions alone.

Another part of the health discussion includes the caregiving that we may need to do for each other. Some studies show that eighty-eight percent of us will need to provide significant care to our ailing spouse for an extended time.[2] The Rosalyn Carter Institute estimates that because of the stresses that caregiving can put on a spouse, one-third of them will decline in health and age prematurely.[3] Providing this care can cause sleep deprivation, immune system deficiency, depression, chronic anxiety, loss of concentration, and premature death.

Joy remembers when she realized that something was happening to her husband, Jim. They were returning from a trip to see an adult child, and he couldn't find their car in the airport parking lot. After some time riding around with a very patient shuttle driver, they located the car. Jim then jumped out of the shuttle, ran to the car, and drove off without Joy or their luggage. Eventually they found each other, and Joy offered to drive home. Jim refused and made a number of wrong turns on the way. Joy knew then that her life would never be the same.

When she shared this experience with their children and family doctor, they all thought she was making too much of it, suggesting that Jim was just fatigued. But these kinds of experiences with disorientation increased, and eventually Jim was diagnosed with Alzheimer's disease. It was not easy for Joy to assume responsibility for their finances and to make the decisions about the future of Jim's business. But it was important for her to do what she could to preserve Jim's dignity. As Jim lost more of his cognitive abilities and became confused, Joy wrote things on cards, such as *cut toenails, I am Joy, sit, eat dinner,* and so forth. The printed words seemed more comforting to him than spoken words. Clearly, what was being communicated was her love.

Lester's parents still lived alone in their old, two-story farmhouse when they were in their nineties. Family members became concerned that the parents weren't caring properly for each other. But when the family talked about help with day-to-day responsibilities, the mother insisted that she could take care of things by herself. Eventually, at the persistence of the family, they agreed to have someone come to help with bathing and meals. In spite of that, Lester's mother got up at four a.m. and bathed herself and her husband, and prepared breakfast, before the caregiver arrived. She and her husband were sitting in their favorite chairs waiting when the worker knocked on the door at seven a.m. It took a medical crisis to convince the parents that they were no longer able to provide adequate care for each other.

Conversations about finances

Long before retirement most of us begin preparing financially for our senior years. We estimate our monthly benefits from Social Security, pensions, and our own investments. At the same time, we try to anticipate our expenses. It is common for us to begin this conversation in our mid-forties, knowing that it is urgent that we begin an investment program. Many of us consult with financial advisors to help make the right plan. Although we talk together about finances, it is typical that one of us plays the treasurer role throughout our marriage, paying the bills, doing the banking, and generally keeping the spouse informed about finances. By the time we begin retirement, we should both be fully aware of our financial situation and be able to look after our day-to-day financial affairs.

In spite of having planned well, we may find ourselves struggling financially. Our investments may have declined, or we may have unexpected expenses. We may have differences of opinion about how to spend our money. One of us might like to travel more, eat in restaurants frequently, or have hobbies that are expensive. We may differ over how much money to give to church or charity or an adult child who may be dependent on us. The greatest challenges may come if we have significant medical expenses. These are difficult conversations that can create tension. It is helpful when we are open with each other and plan for the many "what ifs" that could happen.

Conversations about housing

When we retire, most of us will be living in the same house where we've lived for many years. We are familiar with it, comfortable with the neighborhood, and have many good memories there. In many ways, it has been a sacred space for us. But its size, layout, and features were set up for different circumstances, like raising children.

Talking about moving can be a difficult conversation. Our home can have a different meaning for each of us, and we may be at different points regarding our needs. We may want freedom from care of the property or housecleaning chores. Apartments, condominiums, gated communities for people over fifty-five, and retirement communities with attached nursing facilities begin to look appealing.

But we may not be ready to downsize because we are still enjoying hosting family dinners and want a place for the grandchildren to play. Now that we are freed from the demands of work, we are actually enjoying lawn care, gardening, and minor maintenance. We know that if we move, it will inevitably mean a great deal of disruption, the sale of furniture, cleaning out the attic, changing addresses, and other things which may seem premature or overwhelming.

Knowing *when* to move is perhaps the hardest part of the decision. Many people wait until circumstances force them to do so. Then, often one spouse has to make the decision alone. After Jean had a stroke and was moved to a long-term care facility, John sold their home and moved in with their daughter. Jean now cries about losing her home and not being part of the decision. They should have had the discussion earlier. The process works best when it is begun at the beginning of retirement—or even before.

Companions to the end

As we enter retirement, many of us reflect with some satisfaction on what we have accomplished and feel sadness for failures and losses. We aren't ready to take a seat on the proverbial rocking chair or resign to a life of insignificance. We can still make strong contributions to our family, church, and community. Making new discoveries that keep our marriage fresh is still possible. As companions on this stage of the journey, we will nudge, encourage, and support each other.

For people of faith, the covenant we made with each other on our wedding day has been a source of stability. Faith continues to challenge us to be a "light on a hill." For some, that light illuminates the way for adult children, grandchildren, and other travelers. Even in our senior years, we don't take a sabbatical from this calling.

As we age, we become increasingly aware of our promise to stand by each other in sickness and in health. We know that we are moving inexorably toward a loss of health and that one of us will die first. Our sacred companionship knits us together on a journey that is painful but unavoidable. As our bodies begin to fail, the stronger spouse supports the weaker. As our minds weaken, the one with greater awareness is a source of reality to the other.

Although our adult children can be a vital system of support during this time, we must, if we can, be first responders for each other until the end. We do that even if a spouse is living in a nursing facility and may not know we are there. Our marriage has been a journey. As long as we can, we want to remain beside each other. We have a sacred companionship.

Ending thoughts

Though we may have been married for a long time, none of us has had a *senior* marriage before. Now we face circumstances that we haven't had to deal with before. Our marriage has been driven by our commitment to being good parents, by our careers, the need to pay bills, and our wish to maintain a comfortable lifestyle. Even though we had many good moments together, our focus was often elsewhere.

Now, in many ways, it is just us. We are no longer onward and upward people. As we refocus on each other, we will need to discover new identities, purpose, and a new use for our time and abilities. We will want to show each other special grace during this time of transition and uncertainty. We see each day as a gift, a time of open sharing about new joys and troubling concerns about the future. The day is coming when we will need to care for each other. Already we are helping in ways we didn't before. Intimacy is beginning to take on a new and deeper meaning.

Conversation Starters

- Set aside time each week to talk about how retirement and aging are affecting your relationship.

- Explore new activities that can enrich your time together.

- Discuss how much time to spend together and how much to spend apart.

- Expand daily expressions of gratitude and support.

Questions

1. What keeps you from talking about the changes that will come?

2. How has retirement affected you and your spouse differently?

3. What new skills are important for each spouse to develop?

4. How can each of you help to resolve any differences between the two of you?

CHAPTER 4

Adult Children Consider Their Parents' Aging

DAUGHTER: *Did you know that our friends' parents just moved to a retirement center? They're only a little bit older than Mom and Dad. I don't think I'm ready to see our parents surrounded by old people, thinking that they can't take care of themselves anymore.*

Can you imagine seeing them getting on the home's bus to take them to a concert? Or playing cards to pass the time?

But I do think about what would happen if one of them got sick—maybe had a stroke. I know I couldn't take care of them. I'm plenty busy with my job and running our three kids around.

SON: *It does seem like our relationship with them is changing. Right now I don't feel responsible for them, but I know it won't stay that way. That's probably why they've invited us to a family meeting to talk about*

*their future. They said it is about what our relationship
with them should be as they get older—especially about
their finances and their health, and where they should
live in the future. They even want to talk about the
papers they signed to not keep them on respirators and
IVs when they're near death. But I don't know if I'm
ready for this. It feels too much like switching roles.*

As adult children, it isn't easy to think about our
parents becoming older—to imagine them with weaker
bodies, slower minds, and being dependent. Until now,
it has rarely crossed our minds, mostly because our
parents have always been active and healthy, and we've
been busy with our own lives.

But we can't avoid the subject much longer. We get
some idea of what is coming our way when we read
about a survey showing that forty percent of us will
provide care to our parents at some point. Of that number, sixty percent will be daughters, primarily giving
personal care and home management assistance to
our parents, while thirty percent will be sons, helping
mostly with legal and financial needs. According to the
survey, we will be, on average, forty-six years old when
the caregiving begins.[1] That means many of us will still
have at least one child at home, and about half of us will
be working full-time while providing twenty hours of
unpaid care to our parent.

We also read Gail Sheehy's report that says forty-
three and a half million Americans serve as unpaid
caregivers to an older family member. Because of these

demands, one in six family caregivers lost their job in 2009, and twenty percent of parents share housing with a family member to save money.[2] These numbers have a way of getting our attention.

This call to begin intensive parent care often comes as we anticipate freedom from child-care responsibilities, becoming empty nesters, and not having to care for anyone. Instead, we become part of the sandwich generation.

David was faced with these circumstances. He and his wife, Karen, were fully focused on their nineteen-year-old daughter and their fourteen-year-old son. Although David had known that his father was having leg pain and was being evaluated by several doctors, he found it hard to see, on a Christmas visit, the man who was once so strong and healthy now sitting in a wheelchair. It was even harder when David learned that his father was diagnosed with cancer.

Over the next seven months, David, his parents' only living child, accepted his role as caregiver. He occasionally set aside work and family responsibilities to drive seven hours to be with his father when he was receiving treatment. Karen made the trip on alternate weeks to support her mother-in-law. Following his father's death, David and Karen made additional trips to comfort David's mother and help her plan for the future.

At an early age, Maureen sensed that at some point in her life she would become her parents' caregiver. That sensitivity may have been instrumental in her choosing a nursing career. In spite of that, she was not prepared to begin that role when her father had a heart attack at age fifty-two. She was twenty-five and had two sons, ages two and four. She remembers asking an aunt, "How will I be able to give care to my father and still care for my young children and work?"

"You just have to do it," the aunt replied.

Over the next eight years, Maureen was her parents' primary on-call responder and caregiver. A sibling would help when visiting. In reflecting back on the care she gave her parents, Maureen has no regrets and would do it again. She and her husband, Al, a caregiver to his parents, learned to be more patient, compassionate, and forgiving. They see the model they established with their parents reflected in their sons.

Conversations with our siblings

When we step back from the situation that we're in, we realize that our time of being overloaded will come to an end sooner or later. We also take some comfort from knowing that the model we are demonstrating to our children may influence the way they relate to us when we need care. We recognize that being a healthy, compassionate adult means being open to caring for our own family members.

It is important to plan ahead with our siblings to meet our parents' needs and divide up the responsibilities that we are assuming for them. It is only logical that each of us takes on the responsibility with which we are the most comfortable and have the greatest skill.

Because more of us today come from small families and have left our home communities, caregiving is more challenging. So it is even more essential to meet early in our parents' retirement years to talk about how we will share the responsibilities. The sibling who lives closest or is single may be expected to do more, fair or not. If we have no siblings, we may need to ask for help either from our parents' church or from an agency that works with seniors.

Mary stayed near home and assumed a great deal of responsibility for her parents. She had many siblings, but most of them had moved away. She took leadership in scheduling a family meeting to talk about sharing the responsibilities. As a result, one sibling volunteered to be executor, one to handle the parents' finances, and one to do research on the kind of services available in their parents' community. The siblings who lived close by offered more hands-on care. They checked in with each other regularly about gaps in the care plan.

Lamar's two sisters took primary responsibility for the physical and emotional care of their aging parents. He handled his parents' finances, and his brothers helped with the property maintenance. Because of the extra amount of time his sisters gave to their parents, Lamar gave each of them $1,000 after their parents died. In a similar way, Janet's brother acknowledged the special care that she gave their mother in the months before her death by publicly thanking Janet and presenting her with a rose during the funeral service.

Fortunately, most of us can work out a plan to meet our parents' needs. Typically, one sibling emerges as a leader who is supported by the other siblings. Most siblings are aware that primary caregivers need respite to preserve their own health. However, if siblings don't offer that help, the primary caregiver should request it—sometimes for specific tasks, as well as asking for time off. It's important for the leader to communicate regularly with the siblings and to keep them actively engaged in all decision-making.

Family conflict

Unfortunately, some of us have problems working on a care plan for our parents because we didn't have a good relationship with them earlier in life. Perhaps we are angry about the way they treated us over the years. Our parents might have been detached, and we now find it difficult to show compassion to them. On the other hand, we may have trouble caring for them because we have always been dependent on them and don't know how to change roles now when they need help from us.

Making a care plan can also be difficult when we don't get along well with siblings. If a sibling appeared to be favored by a parent or was domineering, it can interfere with relationships. The youngest siblings may feel like their ideas still aren't respected.

Whatever our situation, it may be helpful to seek a counselor or mediator early in the process to allow the care plan to move forward. When our parents begin to decline, especially if there is a crisis, our relationships will be under even more stress.

Other complications

The care plan is also made more difficult if our parents are divorced. We can be caught between divorced parents who may still be at odds with each other. If we view one parent as "at fault" and the other as the "victim," we can find it difficult to know how to reach out to the at-fault parent, especially if we have not reconciled with that parent. We may reject that parent because of what s/he "did to all of us." On the other hand, we may need to guard against overprotecting the parent we see as the victim. If we ourselves are divorced, the situation can become even more complicated.

If either or both of our parents remarry, our caregiving often becomes more confusing. Sometimes a stepparent can see us as an intruder or may identify us with our other parent. The love that we feel for a parent can be clouded by our ambivalence toward a new spouse. Our loyalties can be divided and confusing. We might feel awkward about our role—especially when the new stepparent begins to decline and may need assistance from us.

Finding forgiveness

If we have experienced any of these painful circumstances, it can be helpful to take the initiative to make peace. There is still time to talk and pick up from where we are now. It may not be necessary to go back over wounds that have become embedded in our memories or to expect complete healing. In fact, reopening old wounds may make them more difficult to resolve. What is important is to forgive each other for past hurts and accept each new day as a gift.

When Angie's mother was diagnosed with cancer, she felt some urgency to reconnect after years of estrangement. She wrote a note to her mother, describing happy childhood experiences and thanking her for those memories. The spirit of the note opened a window that allowed the women to share stories and learn more about each other. They never said the words "sorry" and "forgiveness," but the renewed connection between mother and daughter was profound and brought a deep sense of peace.

Amy often sat by her mother's bedside in the last year of her life. Amy decided to forgive her mother for the emotional abuse she had experienced over the years. Amy took that step even though her mother hadn't asked for it. She realized that her mother probably didn't even know that she had hurt Amy. She felt compassion for her mother and was able to say she loved her. To Amy's great surprise, her mother said, "I love you, too!"—something Amy had never heard growing up. Now that her mother has died, Amy carries no more resentment. Her father was influential in her life and taught her to accept persons she might not like. A phrase that he learned from an African American friend—"Aren't they one of God's children?"—has been helpful to Amy.

Forgiving parents is not easy. We must set aside past hurts and accept them as they are today. We need to believe that parents did the best they could in their circumstances. As parents ourselves now, we, too, make mistakes and will need our children's forgiveness. When we forgive and reconnect with our parents, we offer a wonderful model for our children and grandchildren.

If we have had conflict with siblings, it is helpful to make peace with them as well. If we don't do so while our parents are alive, it may be more difficult to accomplish after their death because siblings tend to go their own directions. That happened with Les, who was estranged from his siblings for most of his adult life. His family rarely got together and, when they did, the brothers never talked. When Les died unexpectedly in his early sixties, a brother who attended the funeral was emotionally moved by the tributes he heard about Les. That allowed him to set aside his anger. He expressed regret that he and Les hadn't reconciled, and he didn't even remember what had caused the estrangement.

Caregiving plan

If we are at peace with our parents and siblings, it will be far easier to develop a plan for the care of our parents. Here are things to keep in mind:

- *Observing*

    We need to become another set of ears and eyes for our parents, beginning early in their senior years. We may be more objective about the early changes in them than they are able to be. Typically, parents aren't objective about the gradual changes happening to them and may even cover up for each other. Sometimes friends alert us to changes that they see. Only then might we begin to notice some tentativeness in their driving, a decline in their housekeeping standards, or bruises that they can't explain.

- *Approaching them about our concerns*

  Obviously we need to be sensitive and supportive as we search together for answers. Many parents are resistant if we suggest that they need help. Asking them questions may be more effective than making statements that may sound judgmental to them.

- *Coordinating their care*

  Eventually we will assume responsibility for our parents' care. It can be helpful to form a team relationship with their medical doctor, staff at an agency on aging, members of their faith community, and others who are likely to be involved in their care. Though the need for care is minimal during the earliest stages of decline, it is helpful to establish this process before the needs become greater.

- *Advocating for parents*

  We should ensure that the services our parents need are available. This may require completing paperwork and accompanying them to

interviews or appointments. Sharing your observations and asking questions can be helpful to
the provider.

- *Providing some direct care to parents*
  This is especially likely for those of us who
  live in the same community as our parents.
  Direct care can include transportation, monitoring medications, and grocery-shopping. The care
  may be as simple as emotional support given
  through visits, phone calls, and emails. Words
  and expressions of comfort are the most basic
  kinds of care. As our parents' conditions decline,
  our direct involvement will increase, tending
  more to their daily needs or ensuring that services are in place. Even those of us who live in
  another community will want to increase our
  involvement through phone contact and more
  frequent visits.

- *Managing their lives when they cannot care
  for themselves*
  This transition is especially difficult if our parents resist our help. But if our conversations with
  them have been ongoing and cooperative since
  the beginning of their senior years, the transition
  will be much smoother as they decline mentally
  and physically.

- *Creating an agreement that outlines our parents' wishes*

  Agreeing on how decisions are to be made provides a reference point when difficult choices confront us later on. That agreement gives us peace of mind when, for example, the car needs to be sold or we begin to manage their checkbook. Having this previous agreement is especially vital for making medical decisions.

- *Caring for ourselves*

  Our self-care is important, especially if we are heavily involved in the day-to-day care of parents. The average time that an elderly parent requires caregiving is five years. But we don't have to assume all of the responsibilities for our parents. Statistics show that many of us wait three or four years before asking for help from siblings or agencies. Sharing responsibilities and engaging community services is important. Stating clearly what level of care we are each able to give helps siblings to share responsibilities. To keep our parents engaged, especially if they are forgetful, write them a note saying *when* we will call or visit. (See Exhibit A on pages 206–207.)

The emotional impact of getting involved

Getting involved in the care of our parents will affect us emotionally, especially as they become more dependent. We can never be fully prepared to parent our parents. Our emotions may cause us to hold back or seek to transfer responsibilities to someone else—a lawyer, a doctor, or the nurses in a care facility. What we cannot escape, though, is that our parents need us to play a primary role in their care. Many of us believe that we have a moral responsibility to ensure that their needs are met.

Whether our involvement with them happens quickly or over many years, it is never easy to see our parents decline. We are sad when we see them walking more slowly or with canes and walkers. Their once strong voices weaken, and they strain to hear what we are saying. It's not easy to see food stains on their clothes or confront odors from a dirty bathroom when we help them shave or comb their hair.

If they are in a nursing care facility, we likely have mixed feelings when we visit. On the one hand, we are relieved that they are getting the physical care they need, that the staff is pleasant, and the facility bright and clean. On the other hand, we dread entering halls filled with people who may be worse off than our parents.

It is especially hard to sit by helplessly when the mind of a parent weakens too soon. Greg's father, Jim, had always been a high energy, outgoing businessman—optimistic even until his death. He was physically strong and athletic. When Greg's mother first mentioned that she was noticing some forgetfulness and disorientation in Jim, he and his siblings minimized her concerns. No one wanted to accept this change in their father. When Jim's health declined further, the family supported admitting Jim to a nursing care facility. It was difficult for Greg to watch as Alzheimer's disease progressed in Jim.

One of their most painful moments came when the family celebrated Jim's seventy-ninth and final birthday. The grandchildren had made birthday cards, only to witness him tear them up as he opened them. It was especially difficult for Greg to comfort his six-year-old daughter and explain why Grandpa tore up, in her words, "the most beautiful card I had ever made." It was impossible to prepare for this moment.

Lois, who lived a two-hour drive away from her parents, began increasing her visits after her father had a stroke. Her mother cared for him for fifteen years until she could no longer do so. Then both were admitted to a nursing care facility. Within months, her mother died, and Lois made even more trips to be with her father. She was able to spend several days with him on her visits, providing some well deserved respite for her brothers and their spouses who lived nearby.

Her father, a once strong farmer who could throw fifty-pound bales onto a hay wagon, now struggled to sit erect in a wheelchair. The stroke had left him unable to speak, but he came to life when Lois sang with him. With a twinkle in his eye, he recalled, with

Lois' help, hymns from hundreds of church services he had attended throughout his life. As he neared death, these songs became the recessional by which he left this world. Lois and the extended family helped to sing their father into a new life.

Kristen was in her thirties when she began to talk with her retired parents about moving from their home in Oregon to her community in Pennsylvania. She wanted them to be able to enjoy her children as they were growing up and to have her parents' support during this demanding time of her life. Kristen also knew that if they stayed in Oregon, she couldn't be much help to them as they aged.

In the eight years since they moved, the benefits have been greater than anyone expected. Kristen has the satisfaction of seeing her parents interact with her children, attend some of their activities at school and church, and babysit when she and her husband, Johncey, need a night off.

Since the move, Kristen and her parents have had medical problems that required surgery. Being in the same community has made it possible for them to care for each other. Most of all, a system of support is now in place for the future.

Grace, a retired teacher from Florida, spends a large part of the year in Pennsylvania, caring for her ninety-one-year-old widowed father. He doesn't want to go to a continuing care facility, preferring to die at home. Grace is committed to his wishes. Occasionally her four siblings provide relief, allowing her time off to return home briefly.

The siblings have developed a meaningful relationship while carrying out their father's wishes. Grace is grateful for the opportunity to care for her father and believes that she is getting more than she is giving. An extra bonus for coming to Pennsylvania is that she can spend time with some childhood friends.

Ending thoughts

When our parents retire and are in good health, we can easily avoid thinking about their futures. We are preoccupied with our own lives, and our parents seem comfortable in theirs. We know that at some point, we should talk with them about inevitable changes, but no one is eager for that discussion. We feel a bit awkward because it seems like *they* should be taking the initiative.

In the beginning of our parents' senior years, our job typically is relatively easy. We notice small changes. One or both of them might be on several medications, but it isn't hard to check with them about how they are doing. Taking them for cataract surgery isn't a major inconvenience. Helping Dad trim the trees or finding someone to mow the yard takes little effort on our part.

But it won't always be that way. When their decline becomes more significant, our responsibilities will increase. When that happens, we will start to realize what this means for them and for us. Perhaps we won't be able to call our mother for recipes, or she'll show less interest in our children. We will know that we have lost something special when we can't turn to our father for advice about finances. Most of all we know that we are beginning to lose them as parents.

We try to prepare ourselves for the day when we will sit by their sides while they're in pain, when they'll need us to comb their hair, or when they can't remember who we are. When that happens, something within us may want to stay away or to leave. We'll have plenty of excuses for doing just that. We will become profoundly aware that the relationship that we have had throughout our lifetime is being dramatically changed. Soon, all we will have left are memories, and we must focus on a future without these people.

But we don't run—we stay. We hold their hands. We stroke their hair. We sing to them and read them their favorite verses from Scripture. When the time comes, we pray for them to be released from bodies that have failed. Until then, we spend time with them because their bodies are still alive. It would be wrong to abandon them. Whether or not they know it, they need us to be there. Most of all, we need to be there.

We will be filled with gratitude if we have joined hands with our parents many years earlier. Such a partnership prepares us for giving them emotional support throughout this time in their lives. We recognize that they really need us in important ways.

Having been a part of their lives throughout their senior years has also made our lives more complete. Our experience with them is preparing us for the time when our children will become our caretakers during this cycle of living and dying.

Getting started

- As an adult child, take the opportunity to talk with your parents about your shared future.

- Observe their changes and share your opinions about what these changes could mean and what you think they should do about them.

- Listen to what your parents want from you.

- Share with them what you think you can offer them.

- If you have siblings, work together with them and your parents on a plan that is fair and meets their changing needs.

- If you are alone, seek support from extended family, friends, your parents' faith community, and service agencies.

Questions

1. What will you do if your parents won't accept help?

2. What factors limit your involvement with your parents? What can you offer to them?

3. How can you and your sibling(s) work together in developing a care plan for your parents?

CHAPTER 5

Conversations About Finances

MOM: *Some of our friends are buying a place where they can spend the winter in the sun. Now that we're retired, why don't we join them? Maybe they have more money than we do, or their retirement plans are better than ours. But can't we do something a little special? I heard that those double-wides in a mobile home park in Florida are selling cheap. I think we should check it out.*

DAD: *Our 401(k)s have taken a big hit. The last I checked they were down 10 percent. I'm just a little uneasy about spending lots of money right now. I know we're not old yet, but you never know what can happen. Just look at Mark and Marge. They spent money like it would last forever, and then she got arthritis so badly that she has to be in a wheelchair. She will probably have to go to a nursing home. Can you ever have enough money?*

I wish you would take more interest in our finances so you can see what I'm talking about. I know those

papers from the mutual funds are hard to understand,
but I worry what you would do if I suddenly died.

DAUGHTER: *Did you talk with Mom and Dad lately?*
Mom wants to buy a place in Florida and says that
Dad worries too much about money. Now that they
are retired, Mom thinks there should be some rewards
for all their hard work. But what really worries me is
that Mom doesn't know anything about their finances.
Dad does all the banking and pays the bills, and I
don't know what she'd do if Dad died.

SON: *To be honest, I don't have any idea about their*
finances either. They both had good jobs and were
putting money away somewhere. You'd think that they
could take some trips or do something special. But
when I brought up their finances to Dad, he brushed
me off. He said they're okay, but he wouldn't give me
any numbers. I got the impression that he didn't want
me nosing into their business.

By the time we parents retire, many of us have a
degree of financial security that we had not known
before. Typically, our debt is gone. We have our investments in place and retirement plans that provide some
income. We may work part-time to supplement monthly
retirement or Social Security checks. If nothing unexpected comes up, we can look forward to some good
times. Finally—or so it seems—we can relax and take
comfort in what we have accomplished.

Yet most of us are faced with living on a fixed income. Gone forever are the days of pay raises, bonuses, and profit sharing. We can no longer count on extra money from job promotions. We know that we are required to begin withdrawing some of our investments soon after we turn seventy, and that will give us some extra money. But we don't like the idea that we might have to use that money for day-to-day expenses. From our first job to our last, we always expected to earn more money. Those days are gone forever.

Now we have to think twice about large purchases and optional spending. Many of our peers still have outstanding debt when they retire, including mortgages and credit card balances. Nearly twenty percent of us declare bankruptcy.[1] Many of us have less money in savings than past generations. We may worry where the money will come from if our house needs a new roof. And what will happen if we need long-term medical care?

We now have to take a second look at the appeals for money from our alma mater. We drop less money in the offering plate when it goes by on Sunday. With less money to give to worthy causes, we feel some sadness, even guilt. We realize that we have less influence on important causes. Our names are left off the banquet fundraiser lists.

Financially we are facing our future alone. We are left to deal with the consequences of how well we prepared for this moment. In past generations, parents turned to their adult children if they ran out of resources. But most of us don't do that anymore. We can only hope that Social Security and our investments will be enough to meet our needs—maybe for twenty or more years.

Shared responsibility

In some ethnic groups, parents and adult children remain financially interconnected. Bishop Lawrence Chiles says that in his African American community, finances are openly shared within the extended family. There is a belief that what's mine is yours, especially in low- and middle-income families. In these families there are few secrets and a great deal of interdependence. But parents with a degree of wealth have become more private and individualistic about their money. They may be especially wary of other members of the community who might want to be "taken care of" by relatives with more money.

Nereida's family, with its Latin American background, has displayed a great deal of openness about finances, especially when several generations have lived together. They have had no financial secrets. Few ever bothered with wills, perhaps because their assets were limited. After their parents died, most families simply distributed any assets among themselves. Sometimes the process doesn't work well. Nereida's father tried to talk with his adult children about finances but was never able to follow through with his plans. She and Lawrence believe it may take another generation to develop new patterns of handling their assets.

Tony says that in Puerto Rico, it is still customary for adult children to provide for the financial needs of parents who are no longer able to work. After the parents die, the extended family and the broader community help to pay for the costs of the funeral. Many ethnic immigrants to the United States typically send money to support their parents, even if the parents are still working.

Among Amish and conservative Mennonite groups, parents expect to be cared for by their adult children. Typically, parents distribute assets within the family *before* their death.

Beginning the financial conversation

To deal with the financial independence that has separated parents and their adult children for generations, we believe it is important for us to invite our adult children to join us as co-managers of our finances early in our retirement years.

Although it might feel awkward, we think there is benefit in disclosing our entire financial status to them. Asking them for their opinions about our finances might not be easy at first. Even though we may not feel any urgency to begin the process, opening up the books to them now makes the situation much more comfortable later on. Such openness can bring a feeling of partnership and a peace of mind to all of us. Doing so diminishes the chance that misunderstandings and family disputes will happen—especially during a crisis.

Our adult children's involvement with our finances may help protect us from scams, unwise investments, and sales pitches. While those of us over sixty-five are only one-eighth of the U.S. population, one-third of scam victims are seniors.[2] As we age, our brains do not process information as fast, making us more vulnerable to making wrong decisions. We are especially susceptible to bad judgments when we're mentally fatigued late in the day, a time when scammers typically call. Knowing that we can and should run any requests by our children prevents us from making a bad decision. Slowing the process down is an important protection. Adult children can express caution, which might prevent us from making a commitment we regret later.

Difficulties with getting started

In much of North American culture, finances are often kept private, even within families. Money is near the top of the list of challenging conversations between parents and their adult children. Few of us have invited our adult children to become co-managers.[3]

That is particularly hard to understand, considering how frustrated some of us were by our parents' lack of openness about finances. That left some of us struggling to understand their finances when they were in a medical crisis or after death, even though we may have been appointed as their power of attorney. It becomes especially challenging if they have unresolved debts. Those of us who went through this experience vowed that we would never let that happen to our adult children.

Many of us have not changed direction yet. An American doctor trapped in a fallen building during the 2010 earthquake in Haiti shouted out to a reporter, "I've got to get out of here to get my estate in order. My kids will never forgive me if they have to take care of my papers." She probably spoke for many of us.

Reasons some parents hold back

One reason that sharing our finances is difficult is because we want to hold onto our power. Our money can be our security, and we may not want anyone, even our children, to know how much we are worth. It is even harder to take advice from them about what to do with it. Sharing is especially challenging if we haven't built a relationship with them based on mutual respect. Opening up this part of our lives can make us feel vulnerable and weak. It is especially difficult if we made some bad decisions about money in the past, or if we are keeping secrets about how we are now spending our money.

Some of us who have acquired significant wealth may fear that if our adult children know how much we are worth, they will demand some of the money now. Sometimes a child pressures parents to rewrite a will to the child's advantage. When parents have significant estates, valuable farms, or successful businesses, family disputes often develop. Sometimes the assets are distributed unevenly or punitively. Some heirs are slighted or even left out of the will, while other heirs are favored. These kinds of stories are common. Every effort should be made to avoid such conflicts long before parents become incompetent or die.

The battles over the transfer of a family farm to the heirs is one example of an especially challenging situation. Sometimes the farm is offered at a reduced price to one child, perhaps for legitimate reasons. When that child sells it to developers at a profit, the siblings are rightfully offended.

Harry was fortunate to get the family farm at a good price. However, when he sold it to developers many years later, he felt it was only right to share the profit with his siblings. He calculated the fair-market price at the time he purchased the farm, including interest that would have accrued. Needless to say, his siblings were grateful and surprised with his generosity. He can attend family gatherings with no regrets. The family is at peace.

When parents have considerable wealth, excessive generosity to their children can create dependency. These children may never assume adult responsibility. If they are given large amounts of money by their parents, they may squander it and maintain irresponsible lifestyles. The stories of free-spending scions are well known. Many never became legitimate wage earners. In all of these kinds of situations, parents need good legal advice and perhaps the services of a mental health professional.

When we have an adult child who is physically or intellectually challenged, it is important to plan ahead for his or her future. Various survivorship care arrangements can be made with the help of an attorney. Such plans usually name an administrator of the assets, who oversees the child's care. Involving the other siblings in this process is essential.

Challenges from divorce and remarriage

If we experience a divorce, our adult children can be left with some difficult challenges regarding our finances. Divorce typically shatters family ties and loyalties and tends to impact our assets negatively. Often decisions about property are made under pressure and in an adversarial environment. Winning and losing can overshadow our better financial judgment. Adult children tend to be caught in the middle between conflicting parents. That can make their role as co-managers difficult or impossible.

The situation becomes even more complicated if we parents remarry, often blending two families together. If we are young when we remarry, we may create a third family, which can create a financial nightmare for adult children. It becomes especially challenging if one spouse brings more wealth into the marriage than the other, or if prenuptial agreements were not worked out in advance.

Facing increased medical expenses

Because most of us now live well into our senior years, we'll likely face significant medical expenses before we die. A major expense for some of us will be long-term residential nursing care. Estimates are that forty percent of us will be admitted to a nursing care facility before we die.[4] (That estimate includes patients in short-term rehabilitation for joint replacements, for example.)

The average stay in nursing care facilities is two years, commonly costing $100,000 per year.[5] Medicare pays a small portion. If all of our assets are depleted, most facilities accept Medicaid as payment.

Those of us with sufficient funds may choose to enter a continuing care retirement community to assure that a nursing home bed is available, in the facility we prefer, when we need it. Typically, the average entrance fee is around $200,000 per couple.[6] The fee varies depending on the size of the unit chosen and other amenities. There is also a sizable monthly fee. The entrance fees help subsidize the unpaid costs of residents in the nursing care unit.

Various long-term health insurance plans meet some of these costs. The plans can be complex, so it is important to know what they cover. Most have limitations, and the premiums can be costly, especially when we are no longer working. In the words of one financial adviser, "People who really need the insurance can't afford it, and those who can afford it don't really need it." Some insurance companies are no longer writing long-term care policies because of the costs they have to assume.

We believe it is important for us to ask our adult children to help us weigh the costs and benefits of this kind of insurance carefully. When Don and Anna Ruth Jacobs first considered long-term insurance, they discovered that it would be expensive because of their advanced age. This prompted them to discuss the matter with their daughter, Jane, who assured them that when they needed care, they'd have a place in her home. Having seen her parents care for her maternal grandmother in their home for eight years served as a good model for Jane.

Because of the offer from Jane, Don and Anna Ruth then chose a plan that pays some of the costs of in-home professional care. The savings that came from that decision made it possible for Don and Anna Ruth to set up an investment plan that will benefit church agencies and other charities in the future. That is especially remarkable considering that they spent most of their adult lives working for various church programs, including twenty years as missionaries in Africa.

Loss of wealth in the broader society

Historically, wealth has usually been transferred to heirs. Today, though, our generation may have less wealth to pass on. Besides changes in the economy, there are many reasons for this situation. Some of us chose a lifestyle that was beyond our means. Others of us have had medical expenses that depleted our assets. We are also living in a time when fewer of us have farms, estates, or businesses to pass on. All of these changes impact our adult children and the various charities that depend on our generosity. We are just beginning to understand how this will affect the broader society.

Death expenses

Significant funeral costs, often in excess of $10,000,[7] confront all of us. Emotions connected with death can influence us to choose expensive funerals as a sign of honor for the deceased. We may fear that a less expensive funeral will reflect badly on us. Sometimes family members have differences over how much should be spent on the funeral, including whether cremation is appropriate. It is especially important that we begin these conversations with our adult children while we are in good health and before emotions influence the family at the time of our death.

We can begin by:

- Talking about our wishes for our final arrangements.
- Exploring options that match our beliefs and wishes.
- Comparing prices for the services we want.
- Putting our plans on paper.

Death of the first parent

Sometimes we neglect to plan for the financial situation that will arise after the death of our spouse. The older we are when we are left alone, the more help we will need. It is after the death of our spouse that many of us reach out to our adult children for the first time. Often it has something to do with finances. Perhaps our spouse balanced the checkbook or paid the bills. Now we are unprepared to take over this job. It is time to turn to our adult children for support and guidance.

Remarriage

If we remarry, our new spouse may have different assets and spending patterns. He or she may share financial resources differently with adult children. Those differences can create conflict in the new marriage and among the siblings. That is why we must determine before we remarry which assets we will share with our new spouse and which we will keep separate.

In most situations we should consult our adult children and keep them informed, even during the time we are dating, to ensure that we are making wise decisions. Obviously, the older we are when we remarry, the more our children should be involved. Sometimes we remarry because we are lonely and emotionally fragile, and we fail to see the need to make a wise financial plan.

We believe it is essential to work with a lawyer to create a prenuptial agreement. In the best of situations, we should have our adult children remain involved in co-managing our separate and individual funds throughout our new marriage.

Karen and Mike remarried when they were in their sixties. Both had had lost their first spouses some years earlier. Because Karen brought greater financial assets into the new marriage, she and Mike consulted a financial advisor and a lawyer to distribute the assets of their deceased spouses fairly. The plan designated that one-third of Karen's assets would be placed into an income-producing trust for her adult children, one-third would be given to designated charities, and the remainder would be brought into the common household purse for her and Mike's use. They also decided that Mike's assets would go to his children.

Lester and Carrie each had young children from previous marriages when they married. Lester is a business owner, and Carrie became an active partner in the company. It seemed appropriate for their children to share equally in the increased value that accrued during the marriage. Lester and Carrie now share financial information with their children, especially details related to the business. Any inheritance that eventually comes to Lester and Carrie from their parents will be passed on to their respective children.

Creating a financial file

As we begin to include our adult children in our finances we should list:

- All assets, including properties and possessions. Items of particular value, such as heirlooms and valuable artwork, should be appraised.

- Life insurance policies with policy numbers, premiums, and dates of maturity, beneficiaries, agents, and other important information. Remember to include phone numbers and addresses.

- Other assets such as stocks, bonds, mutual funds, annuities, and bank accounts should be noted with appropriate identifiers.

- Additional sources of income, including Social Security and pensions. Records of recent yearly earnings for five to seven years can be helpful.

- All liabilities, including debts, mortgages, membership agreements, maintenance fees, property taxes, credit cards balances, and home equity loans. Account numbers, payment dates, and balances are important to record.

- Access codes and passwords are essential for all accounts.

Give each child a copy of this information. Each should know where to find the original documents.

Having this information at one location gives everyone peace of mind. (See exhibits B, C, and D on pages 208–215.)

At the age of seventy-two, Sam suffered a fatal heart attack while traveling with his wife to a family cabin in the mountains in northern Pennsylvania. Ruth was severely injured in the accident and spent three months in the hospital and rehab centers. Naturally, their three daughters were traumatized, grief-stricken, and left with the heavy responsibility of settling their father's affairs, while providing emotional and practical support to their mother.

One of the tasks that fell to them was making financial decisions. Their father had kept good financial records. But it would have been easier for them if they had been given an orientation to his system. They had some difficulty, for example, tracking down life insurance information, beneficiaries, and other data that was filed in different places. They have since learned how the system works and can now assist their mother in future decision-making.

Things can come to a standstill if our adult children don't have the facts they need or know where to find all the pertinent information. It is important that this information is archived where it is safe and accessible in a place known to our adult children.

It is wise to consult with your attorney about the best place to keep important papers. Regulations vary from state to state about who may have access to a safe deposit box and under what circumstances. It probably is not essential to store photocopies of a will or other estate planning documents in a safe deposit box or a fireproof box. Storing originals there may be a good safeguard, but not all counterparts of original power of attorney documents or living wills should be stored in a locked location, because the family may need prompt access to the documents. Some lawyers suggest that a copy of our wills and advanced directives be stored at home for immediate access.

Marriage and drivers' licenses, birth certificates, and copies of social security numbers can be stored in a firebox or safe deposit box.

The adults(s) whom a parent names as agent(s) in a power of attorney should be informed about where to obtain keys and passwords. When the one who granted the power wishes to pass control to the agent(s), s/he should give the agent(s) the keys and passwords. Some children do not have the skills or perspective to justify giving them access to these documents. If several children have such access, they may take inconsistent actions.

Wills

Many of us have had a will for many years. Retirement is a time to reassess and update it to ensure that assets will be distributed to our surviving spouse as we intend, and that the will strives for an outcome that the children will perceive as fair or tolerable. We should also be sure that charities are represented as we wish.

Some attorneys suggest listing in a memorandum a detailed list of personal and household effects that shall

pass to designated individuals. This memo can be refer-
enced in a will that provides that the latest signed and
dated version of the memo is in control.

A will should name an executor to carry out instructions in the will. In some states the law gives relatives
or beneficiaries the opportunity to be appointed to
administer the estate. If none of them will serve, a court
will choose and appoint a bank to administer the estate
when the will is probated.

The authority held by an agent with power of attorney is defined in the power of attorney document. This
person(s) may be granted legal authority to sign documents, write checks, and make legal and financial decisions on our behalf when we are no longer able to.

Many factors go into the determination of whether
to appoint several persons (and whether each has individual authority, or whether they must act jointly), or
whether the document should appoint one or more
alternates. With express mail and email, it generally is
not difficult to arrange for signatures of someone who
is at a distance, although proximity is convenient.

A person who is nominated as executor in a will has
no authority to act until the person is appointed by the
probate court, which will issue a certificate evidencing
authority to act for the estate of the deceased.

The same or a different person(s) can be designated as
a medical agent who holds power of attorney or medical
proxy for each of us. That person is directed to imple-
ment the instructions in a living will. A living will typically provides that, consistent with such instructions,

the agent shall decide matters for which the living will does not set forth directions.

We encourage parents to be open with their children about their finances and their wishes regarding life-extending medical procedures. That may result in less conflict when a crisis develops, although not necessarily so.

The Physician's Order for Life Sustaining Treatment (POLST) paradigm is designed to improve the quality of care that people receive at the end of life. You may want to ask that your living will includes authority for a health care agent to request a POLST, and then that a designated agent or proxy carries out the instructions.

Estate

Whatever the size of our estate, it is important that we seek counsel from a lawyer and financial advisor about how to manage these resources. We may wish to consult an elder-law attorney, who focuses especially on resource planning at this time in our lives. Independent advice is important for our financial security while we are living and can be invaluable when settling our estates.

Each family releases their assets in their own ways. Most pass a portion of them on to their children in equal shares. Many designate their church or some charity to receive a share similar to that of the adult children. Some children encourage their parents to give a larger portion of their estate to charity because they are doing well financially and don't need a great deal of help.

Planning well for the distribution of assets can result in endless good feelings. We know of one woman who remembers her parents as generous, sharing their financial resources with others, including their children and grandchildren. She especially appreciated that they would check to be sure her children were able to handle a money gift. Her father involved her and her brother in planning for succession in the family business. Her father had lost his mother when he was seventeen, so perhaps that made him more careful to have a plan in place for the time when he would no longer be here.

The family established a foundation so that if the business was sold, some of the proceeds could be distributed to various charitable organizations, church agencies, and community projects over the ensuing years. The parents, their daughter and her husband, and their son and his wife were all named directors to manage the foundation and distribute grants annually. The family members meet quarterly to review the investments and make decisions about the distribution of funds.

With some of their inheritance, the one couple created an account within a larger foundation. It has been in place for more than thirty years and continues a family legacy of stewardship. They say, "It has become part of who we are to share resources with others." It is gratifying to observe how that passion of giving to others is being passed on to their children and grand-children. Their humility and generosity are models for everyone.

Ending thoughts

We live in a world in which money and material assets are necessary to survive. It is clear that we need to have a good financial plan in place that will see us through to our end. As we get older, we will need the help of our adult children to supervise and execute the plan. In one way or another, our adult children will be affected by the way the plan is set up.

Whatever our assets may be, we want to be fair about how they are distributed after our deaths. Perhaps what is most important is that we convey an attitude of stewardship that gives our adult children a positive moral view of money. The goal of many of us is to live in ways that allow us to pass on some of our resources to them and to our church and charities that depend on our beneficence.

Throughout our adult years we need to give much thought to how we manage our resources. We need to try to anticipate the expenses that may lie ahead during our senior years. As longevity in North America continues to increase and our need for expensive medical care grows, many of us will outlive our resources. That makes it important that each of us finds appropriate settings for where we will live and be cared for as we age.

As the national treasury empties, we need to examine the decisions we make about expensive medical care, especially if it promises little in the way of improved health. With a high percentage of health care dollars being spent in the last few months of our lives, we must take another look at end-of-life issues. These are hard subjects to talk about before our deaths, but if we choose well, these decisions can be an important part of our legacies.

Questions

1. What are the benefits of sharing financial information with our adult children when we enter retirement?

2. What should we do if children don't want to get involved in our finances?

3. How can we resolve differences we might have with our adult children?

4. Why wouldn't we want our adult children be a part of a meeting with our lawyer? What would be the benefits?

5. If we want to buy a second home in Florida, why should we seek the approval of our adult children?

CHAPTER 6

Conversations About Where to Live

SON: *I think we've got to talk with Mom and Dad about selling their house. Today when I drove by, I saw Dad up on the roof doing something with the chimney. I know he's only seventy, but he's not as steady as he used to be. And the yard is beginning to look a little bit out of control with crab grass and dandelions. He used to have it looking like a golf course. But every time I mention something to him about moving to where maintenance is provided, he gets defensive. He says we'd have to drag him out of this house, and that grandpa stayed here until he died.*

DAUGHTER: *Mom's the same way. She gets real sentimental when I talk with her about leaving the house. She has all these memories of when we were growing up there. Seeing us off to school, our birthdays, the Christmas trees, and us coming down the steps to open our presents. She can't stand the thought of us not being able to be together there for Thanksgiving. I do worry what would happen to them if they had to move. I know they don't want to go to a retirement community.*

DAD: *I'm really feeling pressure from the kids. This idea that I can't be up on the roof to fix the chimney is silly. I feel as strong as ever, and I know how to handle heights. What do they want us to do? If we get some-one in to do all of the repairs on this place, we'll run out of money. These retirement communities that they keep talking about would drive me crazy. I'd have nothing to do. Shuffleboard doesn't interest me. Can you imagine me going along on bus tours with all those old people? Besides, what would my dad say if I sold the homeplace to someone outside the family?*

MOM: *I don't think they realize what this place means to us. When I tell them about all the memories, they shrug and say, you can't live in the past. They say that they'll still come to visit us wherever we are. As far as the holidays, they promise to have us come to their places. Maybe when they get to our age they'll understand.*

Deciding where to live during our senior years can be difficult. If we live long enough, many of us will reside at several places before we die. Most of us are deeply attached to our homes, and it is hard to think about moving. It is the place where we settled down, raised our children, returned at the end of long days, celebrated birthdays, and mourned the loss of loved ones. For most of us, this home is a repository of important memories. We are reluctant to give it up.

An old song, "Bless This House," acknowledges the sacredness of home by asking for God's blessing on its walls, chimneys, windows, and hearth. In some religious communities, the sacredness of the home is acknowledged with a house-blessing ceremony during which water is sprinkled over the front door as the family moves in. Theologian Walter Brueggemann says, "Place is space that has historical meanings, and where some things have happened that are now remembered and that provide continuity and identity across generations."[1]

Now more than in past generations, we find the decision about where to live in retirement difficult because we have more options and we live longer. Our ancestors died much younger, and the parent who survived usually was taken in by an adult child. In many places, parents live with adult children until they die.

Today most of us have fewer children, and they tend to live in other communities. Moving in with or near them may place a heavy burden on them at a busy time in their lives. Besides, we may not want to leave familiar surroundings, and we value being on our own. It is hard to think about losing some of that independence at this time in our lives. Perhaps most importantly, many of us have the financial resources to choose where to live. Many of the options offer amenities, including nursing care when we need it, that we can't find at home or living with our adult children.

Possessions

We may delay a decision about moving simply because we don't know what to do with our possessions. Most of us have more stuff than we would have room for in a new home. That leaves us with some difficult decisions about what to take, to give away, and to throw away.

Family heirlooms like Grandma's quilt, the grandfather clock, the china, or the old train set all need a special home. We are relieved if adult children or grandchildren want them. It is gratifying to keep things in the family. Sometimes third-generation treasures can have even more value, if not in dollars, at least in legend.

Even after giving many things away, we may still be left with a houseful of stuff. Family members may turn down our offers because their decorating tastes are different than ours. The old china cupboard would look out of place in their home. Sometimes they don't want our stuff because they lack space for it.

Many of us become accumulators and fill garages, attics, and basements with things we no longer use. It is no surprise that storage sheds have become so popular in a lot of our communities. When we move, we face the difficult decision about whether to sell things or give them to charitable organizations. Giving things away can be rewarding. For some people, throwing things away is almost impossible.

We should start sorting through our possessions before we think about moving. Doing so often brings back pleasant memories. Consulting with our adult children and distributing possessions early makes us better prepared for our upcoming move.

New developments that add to our options

It has become increasingly possible for us to remain at home for much longer, perhaps until we die. For many of us, it is a viable option because home-based services are now available. The concept of aging in place includes services like visiting nurses, rehabilitation specialists, hot meals, public transit, and medication delivery. We can hire housekeeping and yard care services and adapt our homes to any limitations that we may have.

Many of these services are coordinated by a local agency that deals with aging and can prevent unnecessary hospitalizations. They may also delay admission to nursing care facilities. In fact, one of the mandates of local agencies who work with the aging is to provide in-home services so that some seniors in nursing care facilities can return to their homes.

A related but independent movement, the Village to Village Network, has sprung up in two hundred communities across the United States. Volunteers provide services such as lawn mowing, transportation, grocery shopping, and other tasks—all in an effort to keep people in their homes longer. By paying an annual fee, members receive access to services through a village coordinator. Villagers receive a list of approved tradesmen who can assist with plumbing, heating, and other maintenance needs. Some have expertise in computers and other electronic devices. Perhaps most important are the social connections forged through shared activities and friendships.

Our Lancaster, Pennsylvania, community has a village called Lancaster Downtowners, with about one hundred thirty members who pay an annual fee of $30. The coordinator is enthusiastic about the concept, but a challenge is to recruit younger seniors to serve as volunteers who provide services to the older seniors. It is encouraging to know that members who are in good health will remain longer in the community with a significant degree of independence.

"Cohousing is a type of collaborative housing in which residents actively participate in the design and operation of their own neighborhoods."[2] The concept began in Denmark in the 1960s and was brought to the United States in the 1980s. The majority of these communities include between twenty and forty households. The neighborhoods are built on small plots of land, making them intentionally intimate. They provide a common room where residents may meet socially and to conduct neighborhood business. Walking and other outdoor activities are usually planned for. Many intentionally invite residents of all ages. One that is in the planning stage in the Lancaster, Pennsylvania, community, Shalom Villages, may have a majority of residents who are sixty-five+, but multigenerational living will be encouraged. The cohousing concept encourages residents to provide each other with social and practical support.[3]

Concurrent with these community-based housing arrangements is the growth of high-tech equipment to monitor our health and safety at home. Call bracelets can bring emergency care, and smart boots alert off-site nurses if we fall. Other technology tracks whether we are taking medications correctly, reducing the high number of seniors hospitalized from medication errors. Other devices that allow medical surveillance in our homes include instruments to measure blood pressure and blood sugar levels. And more are being developed.

Discussing housing with our adult children

Making the right choice about housing is complicated, and the options can be confusing. Our emotions and those of our adult children can be intense when facing these decisions.

Various studies show that eighty percent of us say that we want to stay in our homes as long as possible, but few of us have given much thought to other possibilities. It doesn't seem to be on our adult children's minds either. These conversations should take place in a spirit of mutual respect. All of us will be impacted by the decisions that are made, or not made. The following factors are important to include in our discussions about housing:

- our age
- our health status
- whether both of us are living
- size, condition, and adaptability of our current property
- cost of maintaining the property
- proximity and availability of family
- access to community services
- transportation needs
- our financial status
- personal preferences
- other options

As part of the conversation, it is important to assess safety and mobility features that exist in one's present house and in any future setting. These features include wheelchair accessibility, outside entrances with no steps, and first-floor living that provides both a bedroom and bathroom. These accommodations may reduce the need for seniors to move to other settings prematurely and can maintain aging in place for as long as possible. Dr. Kimberly Stoeckel found in her research that forty-seven percent of persons over fifty-five were unable to identify any possible barriers to safety and mobility in their present settings, when in fact, barriers were present. Of that group, seventy-five percent indicated no plans to move to another place.[4]

Clearly, the healthier and wealthier we are, the more choices we have regarding where we live. Regardless of our status at the beginning of our senior years, though, changes will take place that may make it necessary for us to move. Typically, we'll make several housing changes before we die.

Part of the discussion should include an ongoing assessment of our ability to handle day-to-day matters. Is one of us able to cook, clean, and assume other tasks of daily living? Are we able to provide personal care to a spouse who is ailing? Can we find someone to mow our lawn or provide household services when needed? Can adult children assist the caregiver when demands become overwhelming?

One of the realities influencing housing choices is our financial situation. This is especially critical during uncertain economic times. The value of our homes and investments may have fallen significantly. This loss of net worth will have a direct impact on our decision about where we live. Can we afford continuing care retirement communities and nursing home care?

We need to look at our options, and with our adult children make the best decision.

Option one:
Stay where we are

There is no compelling reason for many of us to leave our homes, especially if both of us are in reasonably good health. We are able either to do the routine maintenance, housekeeping, and other tasks ourselves or pay someone else to do them.

Earl and Vera, now in their mid-eighties, continue to find enjoyment from working in their garden and flowerbeds. Earl gets pleasure from mowing their yard on a riding mower. Vera keeps their property immaculate and their flower gardens filled with variety and color. Weeds cannot be found anywhere. From their living room window, they enjoy the view of the pond on the farm where they used to live. They value hosting many family events in their recreation room.

Many of us find that our homeplace is filled with good memories. It is still a good gathering place for the extended family and for entertaining friends. The familiar grocery store is just around the corner. The doctor's office is a five-minute drive away. Some of us aren't ready to give up our walks through the town park, the church where we have been long-time members, or to move away from our neighborhood friends.

We are able to make changes to the house to make it safer and more accommodating to our needs. We install grab bars in the bathrooms, we put in showers that accommodate wheelchairs, and we remove loose rugs that could cause a fall. We consider installing motorized stair chairs to allow us to move from floor to floor. Perhaps most important of all, we access aging-in-place services in our communities. We also receive some support from our faith community.

Some of us have informal care arrangements with our neighbors. When Menno's wife died, he made an agreement with his neighbor that if his kitchen window shade remained drawn in the morning, she would check to see if he was all right. That plan worked well for a number of years. Later, when his health declined significantly, Menno's family began to provide more day-to-day care.

The availability of family members to give some level of care has a direct impact on our ability to remain at home. Adult children—especially if they live nearby—can check on us from time to time and assist in a variety of ways. But we must recognize that as our health declines, their burden increases, even if we have in-home health services and have hired a housekeeper.

Many of our adult children have careers and children who need them. Adult children who live in other communities often find it difficult to give enough support by phone or on their occasional visits. The challenges increase when both of us parents are no longer able to drive. If we aren't able to find substitute transportation, we can become lonely and lean even more heavily on our adult children.

Option two:
Move to a smaller place

For many of us, the place where we live is really too big and expensive to maintain. Housekeeping is beyond what we can comfortably manage. The yard and other maintenance requirements are too strenuous—maybe even dangerous. Some of us eventually choose to leave our homes because we have lost interest in yardwork, gardens, and house maintenance. Moving to a smaller house, condo, or apartment that requires less care becomes appealing.

Moving to a smaller place allows us to remain in an age-diverse community, maintain independence, and protect our financial assets. We have access to home-based medical and community services. Maintaining independence enables us to continue meaningful connections with our family and friends. Moving to a smaller place gives an opportunity to downscale our possessions.

When John and Janet were sixty years old, they chose to leave the farmette where they had raised their family. They wanted to be freed from the ongoing maintenance the old farmhouse required. Although they are comfortable with their decision, they do miss their beautiful view of the meadow and the privacy of country living.

At first, their adult children weren't enthusiastic about the move, in part because they wanted their children to enjoy the farm as much as they did while growing up. However, now that John and Janet are in a new place that requires less maintenance, they have more time to visit their children and grandchildren. When the family comes together now, they are especially grateful for the finished basement where the grandchildren can play. It has become a good place for their gatherings.

Janet finds it exciting to live in a new house for the first time. She can do more creative decorating. John especially likes the fact that it is easier to clean. They purposely chose a home with less square footage, but because of the design, it somehow feels bigger. The move made it necessary to get rid of some of their possessions, but they found it rewarding to return childhood treasures to their adult children. John and Janet enjoy being in a neighborhood that has a good mixture of families and retirees.

Option three:
Move to a fifty-five+ community

Age-restricted communities sprang up in the Sun Belt several decades ago as retreats for retirees, especially for winter use. In more recent years, they have become year-round residences. This model has since expanded to many other states. While comfort, recreation, low maintenance, and camaraderie with peers are their main purpose, some seniors like the fact that they are protected from the noise and frenzy and crime in the neighborhoods they left behind. Some residents feel even safer when the communities are gated.

Many of these communities have rules that limit the number of days that adult children and grandchildren can stay overnight on their visits. In most situations, the seniors retain ownership of the house but pay a monthly fee for services, including yard maintenance and snow removal. Some associations offer clubhouses that sponsor activities and swimming pools, and some have private golf courses.

Although some residents like the fact that noisy children aren't under their feet, others are bothered by the limitations placed on their families. They may also miss the relationships they had with their previous doctors, friends, and church. Transportation can become an issue if public transit isn't available. If their adult children live in distant communities, the amount of support that they can provide to their parents is limited.

Joanne experienced that situation with her parents, who left their lifelong home in the north to enter a fifty-five+ community in Miami. They enjoyed their senior years in a carefree, warm, and sunny environment for many years. However, when Joanne noticed some cognitive and physical decline in her mother, she knew that the time had come to broach the subject of having them move closer to her. When she brought up the subject, her parents resisted. They were not ready to leave their familiar setting. Joanne remains concerned about assisting them from a distance.

Option four:
Move closer to adult children

Although Betty's parents lived only about fifteen miles from her, the distance became a factor as she began to attend to their personal care and oversee maintenance of their large property. She was increasingly worried about their safety.

Her parents had initially resisted selling their home because they thought it would mean they'd have to go to a retirement community. When Betty suggested that they buy a house close to her, the decision was an easy one. Betty now finds it much more convenient to assist them with their meals, to monitor their medicines, and to look after their other needs. Providing transportation to doctors' appointments and church is simpler as well.

A special highlight for her father is that he can go fishing with Betty's husband, Mike, at a nearby lake. Perhaps the most important gift Betty and Mike give her parents is emotional support and companionship. In addition, they can be part of visits with the grandchildren and great-grandchildren. Betty says she has no regrets despite the added care that she now provides her parents. She knows her parents are content and says, "I wouldn't have it any other way."

Marion and Verna Schrock spent most of their adult years in Oregon. After retirement, they made frequent visits to their daughter and her family in Pennsylvania. Initially they purchased a condo near to Kristen to make it possible for them to stay for extended visits. At Kristen's urging, they decided to make a permanent move to Lancaster. They then bought a larger condo. It provides more space when Kristen, her husband, Johncey, and the three grandchildren come for meals and impromptu gatherings, even for sleepovers. This also provides room for their son and his family from California when they come to visit. It has become a special gathering place for all of the grandchildren to play together.

The move to Pennsylvania was rewarding for Marion and Verna despite the friends and memories they left behind. Now they treasure the opportunity to play a bigger part in the lives of their Pennsylvania grandchildren. Kristen and Verna can and freeze together in the summer. Marion enjoys caring for his grandchildren, helping with car maintenance, and assisting with the upkeep of the property.

At the same time, Kristen has been supportive during their health challenges, including surgery. Marion and Verna have reunited with friends from college, made many new friends, and have found a supportive church community. They are both in meaningful volunteer assignments.

Harold and Gloria Nussbaum made the opposite cross-country move, leaving their home in Pennsylvania to be close to their daughter and her family in Oregon. They were in their early fifties and at crossroads in their careers at that time. They took the opportunity to make changes in their lives. As they thought about how much they were missing their daughter and grandchildren, it only seemed logical to move closer to them.

Harold and Gloria now treasure the frequent times with their daughter and her family, and they enjoy new friendships at their church in Portland. Harold has found a meaningful job in the city, while Gloria has developed a family history recording business in their home. Friends from the East occasionally visit. Interestingly, Harold's mother has followed them to Portland. Four generations now are aging together in the same community.

When Jim began to show significant signs of dementia, Joy knew it was time to consider downsizing. When their son, Greg, invited them to build a smaller house on his property, Joy knew it was the right thing to do. She and Jim enjoyed their new, attractive, senior-friendly home for several years before it became necessary for

Jim to move to a continuing care facility nearby. Joy is comforted knowing that Greg and his wife are close by and enriched by frequent, spontaneous visits with the grandchildren. They stop in for cookies or help with a knitting project. Joy frequently visited Jim at his nursing care facility until he died. Even though Joy and Jim left their longtime home to move next to Greg and his family, they were still close to their church and friends.

Retired mission workers Don and Anna Ruth Jacobs asked their adult children and spouses for advice about long-term health insurance. The questions not only led to a discussion about their finances, it also opened up the subject of where they would live during their senior years. Their daughter, Jane, and her husband, Glenn, who lived about twenty miles away, suggested they would add an apartment to their home for them. This meant that Don and Anna Ruth would only need to purchase in-home health care insurance.

Unfortunately, the zoning board rejected the building plan because it included a kitchen, which by zoning standards made it a multi-family dwelling. When a house next door to their daughter was up for sale, Don and Anna Ruth immediately bought it. In the ten years since that time, everyone—including the grandchildren and now a great-grandchild—are satisfied living close to each other.

Not only does it make good financial sense, but Don and Anna Ruth feel assured that their medical and emotional needs will be monitored by their daughter and their son-in-law, who is a physician. If they need care beyond what the family can provide, their insurance policy will cover much of the cost of in-home agency care.

In the meantime, Jane and Glenn built an apartment in their house for Don and Anna Ruth when they need it. Because it has no kitchen, they will share meals with Jane and Glenn, as they already do from time to time. Presently, the space provides a place for the extended family to gather.

The Jacobs, now in their eighties, look to their future with confidence. Not only do they have a plan that is working, but they also experience daily the pleasure of aging among family. Don takes great pride in his three lily ponds, which bring back memories of the ponds he enjoyed at his home as a child. Anna Ruth likes living in her own home, cooking, and entertaining. The positive, life-affirming attitudes within the family make this housing option possible. In their later years, Don and Anna Ruth continue to live joyfully and with meaning.

Option five:
Adult child moves close to us

Although it is less common, some adult children choose to move to the community where their parents live to support them during this time in their lives. The move may mean returning to the community where they grew up, making it possible for them to renew ties with old friends and reconnect with places they valued earlier. Most find new jobs and are able to develop support systems for themselves.

After I (Gerald) had major surgery, our daughter Anne and her husband, Todd, chose to move back to our community. They wanted to be closer to Todd's parents, too, allowing them and us to be more actively involved with their three children.

Todd has retained his dental practice in their former community, despite having a significant commute. The entire family is convinced that they made the right move at the right time. Anne has developed a professional coaching career in their home. It has been helpful to us and our children to be part of our support network. Our family gatherings have become rich times of bonding. Although we are in good health presently, the family knows that will change eventually. Their presence in our community is reassuring.

Brian Castner, in the "My Turn" section of *Newsweek* in March 2007, wrote that when he ended his career in the military, he and his wife had to decide where to put down roots and raise their three sons. At first the most important criteria included living where there were trees and green grass, preferably somewhere in the eastern United States. They were tired of living in places around the world that had brown landscapes.

It eventually occurred to them that what they really wanted was for their children to grow up near their grandparents in Brian's hometown of Buffalo, New York, where they would also be near great-grandparents, aunts, uncles, and cousins. Brian realized he had taken his large supportive family for granted until this point. Some of his friends didn't understand why he wanted to move home. They said that they had seen too much of the world to move back to what they considered to be a small, predictable, boring town. Brian's reply was, "I have seen too much of the world *not* to move home."

Option six:
Three-generation living arrangements

Several generations ago it was common for parents, adult children, and grandchildren to live in the same house, especially after one of the older parents died. That pattern is still common among some ethnic groups in the United States—especially with Hispanic, African American, and Asian families. In many of these situations, the only privacy parents have is in their own bedroom. They spend most of their time with the family. Living together may reflect economic necessity, but it is also a pattern that extends from their original home countries, where the old are highly regarded and an integral part of the family.

Bishop Lawrence Chiles says about African American households, "We have our own version of the *grossdawdy* house. We just live in the same house—it doesn't matter how many people are there. There's always room for one more. The older generation helps to take care of the younger generation." When the parents' health declines, the roles are reversed, and the adult children become caregivers. In each of these shared housing arrangements, there is a great deal of interaction among the generations. Aging is seen as normal, and the life cycle from birth to death is a part of everyone's daily experience.

Although there are few statistics on how many families live in some kind of shared household arrangement, there appears to be renewed interest in this practice in the broader society. This change in attitude may be driven by economic pressures, especially those coming from the high costs of institutional and medical care. It may also come from an increased awareness of the value in multigenerational family living. After many decades in which American families have scattered to distant locations, this trend—if it is one—is encouraging. It demonstrates that for many families, three-generation households can work.

Helena and Patrick began talking with her parents when they were in their fifties, about moving in with them when her parents needed care. During one of those conversations, her father asked, "What are we waiting for?" Even though they were somewhat surprised, Helena and Patrick responded, "Why not now?" They moved soon after this discussion.

They eat most meals together. The living room, dining room, kitchen, and family room are all shared space. Everyone helps with cooking, cleaning, upkeep, and lawn care. They share household responsibilities, as well as tools and equipment, and everyone contributes to the household finances. They say that the benefits for the grandchildren and the adults are too numerous to put on paper. They are all happy to be a part of this arrangement, especially while the grandparents are still relatively young and active.

Families move together at different points in their lives and for differing reasons. When John and Myrna were putting an addition onto their farmhouse, it seemed like the perfect time to include a *grossdawdy* apartment where Myrna's parents could live. At first it was difficult for them to think of leaving their home-town in Ohio to move to Pennsylvania.

They eventually decided to move because they were in their late seventies, and neither of their daughters was close by. They made an agreement with John and Myrna to pay for two-thirds of the cost of adding on the apartment. In hindsight, John and Myrna feel that there should have been more clarity about the financial arrangement and that a written memo would have been helpful. But it worked well for everyone. Myrna's parents lived with the family for twelve years. Toward the end of their lives, they each had short stays in skilled care facilities. The money left in their estate was evenly distributed to the adult children.

Harold and Mary realized it was time to turn over the farm to one of their sons and his family. Harold and Mary explored the possibility of entering a retirement community. Their other son, Steve, along with his wife, Marilyn, had already begun making plans to build a house on the property for their family. When Marilyn heard about her in-law's intentions, she suggested that an apartment be added onto the house for them. Harold and Mary were surprised by the offer. They were pleased to remain among family members and in a neighborhood that was special to them.

Marilyn designed an attractive house that, in addition to the in-law quarters, has a large common room in the basement. It has become a wonderful place for the forty extended family members to gather for special occasions. The entire family is pleased with this arrangement. After eleven years, nobody has any regrets.

Robert and Lois Kreider relate the following story about shared housing:

> For twenty-five years, Lois and I lived on a farmstead leased from Bethel College. Adjacent to the campus, the farmstead consists of a frame house built in 1915 with a hip-roof barn, shop, chicken house, storage shed, barnyard, and white wood fence fronting on Main Street. The cluster of buildings is protected from north winds by a row of Osage orange trees planted more than a century ago. Behind the farm buildings runs Kidron Creek, much of the year a trickle, but after downpours a raging flood.
>
> West of the creek is Kidron Bethel Village, a retirement community. Our neighbor Harold rents space in the barn and farmyard for his five handsome Arabian horses. Behind the barn along the creek can be seen the swale of the rut marks of chuck wagons on the Chisholm Trail, along which, in the years 1867-1871, a million Texas longhorn cattle were driven to the railhead at Abilene, sixty miles north. This place has linked us to our rural past: gardening, planting trees, sharing the property with squirrels, opossums, raccoons, foxes, turkeys, and an occasional beaver and deer.

In 2003, our son David and wife, Heidi, and our daughter Karen and husband, Steve, purchased the farmstead from the college. Not long thereafter, when Lois and I were considering a move to a duplex in the nearby Kidron-Bethel Village, David approached us. "I would like to spend an evening with you talking about an alternative." Supported by others in the family, he proposed to build an addition for Lois and me. David, Heidi, and sons Benjamin and Mark would live in the main house. The idea clicked.

David busied himself in creatively designing an apartment addition with an open layout for a kitchen, dining room, and study, together with bedroom and bath, porch and ramp, and a guest suite above the garage. Our two families share a family room between the apartment and main house. At Thanksgiving we have seated about twenty people at a long table, the dinner served out of the two kitchens. We also share magazines and newspapers, garage, laundry, freezer, storage space, guest rooms, garden, and many services.

We share frequent meals, guests, surprises, and delights. We hear Mark practice his Bach and Beethoven on the piano. We tap Ben for his computer expertise. The two often join us to share their school triumphs. After high school soccer games, six of us may gather at our table for ice cream and soccer talk. Lois and I think this intergenerational living is adding years to our lives—certainly, stimulation and pleasure. And we live on the edge of Bethel College's campus with its flow of stimulating activities.

Option seven:
Continuing care retirement community

Some of us enter a continuing care community to simplify our living and put behind us the responsibility of maintaining a home. Typically, these communities have a full range of housing choices, including condos, cottages, and apartments. The residents join a community of peers where conversations and activities are compatible with their stage of life. Most communities provide stimulating activities, lectures, and concerts. Many have recreational facilities such as indoor swimming pools, exercise rooms, woodworking shops, and hiking trails. At first glance they look very much like college campuses. People who choose these communities find new purpose and supportive friendships. They feel relieved from the burden of caring for a home.

Dick and Ruth chose to downsize and move into a retirement community in their early seventies. Now that they have fewer things to care for and no property to maintain, they have more time to appreciate what is important to them: friends, reading, enjoying creation, and spending more time with their grandchildren. It also gives them satisfaction to realize that disposing of possessions and selling their property will not burden their children in the future. Nor will the children be responsible for their medical needs later in life.

The children host most large family gatherings. However, they frequently come to the retirement community to share Sunday meals with Dick and Ruth. These meals are served in one of the campus dining rooms.

Family holiday events can be held in a large community room with a kitchen, piano, and comfy upholstered furniture. The younger grandchildren quickly adapted to the new opportunities for play, including more space to ride bikes and scooters, a swimming pool, and a playground.

Perhaps the biggest attraction that these communities provide is the presence of nursing care for medical problems or continuing needs. This brings a sense of security to those who live there and their children. Staying within the campus provides a feeling of continuity. When one's health declines, it becomes increasingly important for adult children to visit and give emotional support. Depending on the level of care needed, they may take their parents to doctors' appointments and to off-campus family gatherings. When that is no longer possible, children's visits, walks down the hall, and shared meals in the dining room can be enriching. While the staff is able to meet many of the residents' physical needs, they can't take the place of family. Some adult children visit their parents several times a week. This is especially important as parents begin to lose their health.

One drawback for some people, especially in their earlier senior years, is that these communities lack age diversity and other aspects of typical community living. One author refers to them as "elder islands." Although residents have contact with the outside world when they leave campus, most of the time they are around people their own age. Retirement communities can be places of more sunsets than sunrises.

One of the advantages that continuing care communities provide is the assurance that a nursing care bed will be available when needed. Some facilities only admit their own residents to the campus nursing care facility.

Many nursing units are now designed around the *household* concept, which provides a homelike setting for residents. Instead of a hospital environment with long halls, prominent nursing stations, call bells, and large dining rooms, the units are smaller and more intimate. The visual and auditory distractions are minimized. Nurses' stations are almost invisible. The environment is much more resident-friendly.

It is hard, of course, to measure the effects these efforts may have on residents, especially those in the end stages of life or with dementia. But residents receiving rehabilitation services or who perceive what is going on around them like the homier environment, as do their families. Such facilities tend to be a pleasant place for staff to work.

Many continuing care facilities provide nursing services to aged people in the broader community through their visiting nurse programs and day-care services for community seniors at the campus.

Option eight:
Independent nursing care facility

Some nursing care facilities are stand-alone operations offering personal and skilled care. They have no cottages, condos, or apartments.

Many of their residents are transferred directly from a hospital following an acute medical crisis. Some receive physical therapy and are able to return home. Studies show that about forty percent of us who are sixty-five and older will at some point have a short stay in a nursing care facility and be discharged to our homes or to the care of relatives.[5]

Many patients are admitted with little chance of recovery. They may have suffered a debilitating stroke or have severe Parkinson's disease or some form of dementia. Many will stay until they die. Women over eighty-five with some level of dementia occupy the largest number of beds in long-term care. The average length of stay for people needing personal and skilled care is about two years.[6]

One common misunderstanding is that you need to live in a continuing care campus to have access to a nursing home bed. When someone is hospitalized for a serious illness and needs continuing care, a hospital social worker will find a bed—most likely in an independent nursing care facility. It may not be the preferred one, but a bed will be available. We may eventually be able to transfer to the facility that was our first choice when a bed becomes available there.

All such facilities are regulated by state and federal agencies and must meet minimal standards for nursing care, nutrition, safety, and basic social needs. If a patient doesn't have the financial resources to meet the costs, most of these facilities accept Medicaid as payment.

As with most medical services, the architecture, aesthetics, and the environment in these facilities vary a great deal. Some are cheerful, attractive units with dedicated staff members. They have in-house activity programs that attempt to create a stimulating and compassionate environment. But many remain hospital-like facilities with long halls and large dining rooms. Regardless of the physical setting, many nursing care facilities have compassionate staff who are skillful at dealing with residents who are in serious decline.

After Millard had a stroke, his wife, Mary, cared for him for many years. When her health declined and she could no longer attend to him, they entered an independent nursing facility. Within weeks of arriving, Mary died unexpectedly, leaving Millard to adjust to life without her and to his new surroundings. Their daughter Lois was impressed with how quickly the staff rallied around her father to bring him comfort. They seemed to understand his needs, even though he couldn't speak after his stroke.

As he approached death, the family, including great-grandchildren who sat on his bed, gathered and sang hymns as he breathed his last breath. The nurses washed his body, placed an embroidered white cloth over him, and escorted Millard and the family to the waiting funeral director. Lois is filled with gratitude for the countless ways the staff went beyond the call of duty to care for her parents.

Ending thoughts

Where we live is important to us. People who have experienced the numbing effects of homelessness or the insecurity of being refugees wish for a permanent dwelling place. Even military or professional families who move frequently can feel loss from not having a permanent place to think of as home. In the backs of our minds—and at the center of many faiths—we understand the earth as a temporary home. But it is natural that we desire some degree of permanency. Although the human spirit can be restless and adventure-seeking, most of us lean toward settledness as we age.

Where we are going to live and die weighs heavily on most of us as we get older. It is difficult to think of giving up our homeplace and potentially our independence. Leaving portends a detachment from neighbors, support systems, and possibly family when we need them more than ever. So it is vital that we have many conversations with our adult children about housing transitions.

Living in a culture that sends its youngest and most vulnerable children into institutional day care, many of us wonder if our society is prone to have our oldest in institutional senior care. While it may be necessary for some of us to be in hospitals and nursing care facilities, we need to explore other options for receiving care in our communities.

Aging in place makes it possible to stay in our homes near the people we care about most. If zoning laws in our communities are out of date, perhaps we should band together to change them to be more flexible in allowing three-generation family living. To keep things fair among our children, and to compensate the adult child who is a primary caregiver, it may be helpful to have an attorney work out an agreement that is acceptable to all parties.

It is important to continue our family story together, to keep in mind that we are developing a family narrative that can be passed to future generations. Good alternatives exist. Families are writing new stories every day. Some involve regular and meaningful visits to parents in continuing care facilities. Some involve close ties between the generations, even though they live in separate locations. Others live near each other or even in the same household. Where we live should be a part of the family conversation.

Questions

1. What can adult children do if their parent(s) are no longer able to care for themselves but refuse to accept help?

2. When parents are still in their own homes and need care, how can each adult child share in caregiving?

3. What are the pros and cons of three-generation living?

4. Isn't it better for parents to be around people their own age?

CHAPTER 7

Conversations About Health

MOM: *I don't know why it is so hard to get my blood sugar down. The doctor said it's still over two hundred. He gave me a little lecture about being overweight and thinks I should set up an appointment with a dietician. But I'm seventy-five, and maybe it doesn't matter anymore. My mom was a lot heavier than I am and had diabetes, too. She lived until she was eighty-three. So maybe it's not such a big deal.*

DAD: *I think they make too much out of all these numbers. We know lots of people who are heavier than we are, and they seem to be doing okay. Sometimes I think doctors have to come up with things just to keep you coming back.*

DAUGHTER: *Mom just called and is upset about the lecture she got from the doctor. He's concerned about her weight and especially her diabetes. I told her that from my experience as a nurse, bad things can happen when diabetes isn't controlled. At first she got defensive and used the old denial thing, like, "I don't eat much cake, and I'm not as heavy as my friends." But when I told her how much the grandchildren would miss her, she softened up and promised she would see the dietitian.*

SON: *Good job! Glad that you can get through to her because I know I can't. My main worry is Dad. Did you know that he's had two fender-benders in the last three months? He says it was the other people's fault, but that's not what the police reports say. I know he doesn't see as well as he should, but he won't go to the eye doctor because he's afraid he has cataracts. Dad never did like the idea of going to the doctor, especially if he thought he'd have to have surgery.*

Many seniors are in good health at retirement, but that doesn't continue forever. At first we are able to remain active and enjoy our new life. Other than taking a few medications to stay well and being more careful when climbing ladders, we feel like not much has changed. So health and safety are not topics high on our list.

We do notice that our older friends are slowing down. Some even have serious illnesses. We read reports that tell us that eighty percent of us will develop a chronic medical condition, and fifty percent of us will have several conditions at the same time.[1] When we read the obituaries, we notice that more people our age are dying!

So it's not *whether* our health will decline but *when*. How will it happen, and what should we do about it when it does? Advances in modern medicine can postpone the decline, but we can't avoid it forever.

From a cost standpoint, most health care dollars in the United States are spent during the last few months of life. The health care burden for people over eighty-five is six times higher than for people between fifty and fifty-four.[2]

Adult children as part of our medical team

If we begin the conversation about health with our adult children before health problems develop, they become part of our medical team. They become partners in our health care decisions. Unfortunately, many of us do not have these conversations until we are in a crisis. Then we are forced to make decisions under pressure. Typically, our adult children don't know what medicines we are taking, who our doctors are, or what health conditions we may have. We don't keep them up to date on our progress or condition.

In a medical crisis, this lack of knowledge may create some guilt in our adult children for not being current about our health. They might think: "If only I had talked more with Dad about exercising." "I wish I had insisted on taking Mom to a dietitian to talk about her diabetes." "If only I had been more observant about his driving." Instead, they now are faced with parents who are incapacitated from strokes, or have sores on their legs, or are in the hospital following a car accident. Some of these situations could have been prevented.

Developing a medical file together

A partnership with our adult children begins by sharing with them all aspects of our health in the beginning of our senior years. If they are going to be helpful partners throughout our remaining years, we should keep nothing from them. Our medical file should contain:

- A list of illnesses for which we're being treated, as well as allergies and past surgeries.

- A list of medications, including dosage instructions and possible side effects.

- Baseline numbers for blood pressure, cholesterol, glucose, and weight.

- Copies of signed consent forms permitting medical providers to release medical information to our adult children.

- Appropriate legal documents about our health, including advance directives that spell out our wishes as we near death.

- The name and phone number of any health care proxy who has the legal authority to govern decision-making.

- The names, addresses, and phone numbers for our health care providers and hospitals. (See Exhibits E and F on pages 216–219.)

Partners in prevention

As the aging process weakens our bodies, there is much we can do to stay well for a long time. To some extent, wellness is a choice, and our adult children can play an important part in keeping us well. Their support can help us avoid or minimize life-changing illnesses and accidents.

Prevention should be a priority in our lives. Far too many illnesses and injuries occur when we simply ignore warnings and advice about staying well and safe. For some reason we think nothing will happen to us. Our adult children can play an important role in keeping us on track. We need their coaching as we get older.

This partnership includes having them accompany us, at least some of the time, to doctors' visits. This could be the time to sign the appropriate paper permitting the provider to share information with adult children. It is helpful when our health care providers have some contact with our adult children before our health declines. Many doctors welcome having younger family members involved as another set of ears and eyes. It makes their job easier if they know that a support person can confirm that we are following the treatment plan.

Proper use of medication

Most seniors take medication to treat various conditions. Failure to take these meds as prescribed can have serious consequences. Pill dispensers are a good way to keep track of medicines. The dispensers help adult children monitor whether we are taking medications appropriately and observe any side effects that might come from a medication.

Many of us are on multiple medications to treat concurrent conditions. In the United States, about fifty percent of us take five different medicines concurrently, while about twenty-five percent take between ten and nineteen medications.[3] Recently, a nurse in a local hospital related that it was not unusual for her to dispense more than twenty different medicines to some of her elderly patients. Obviously, taking multiple medicines at the same time can be confusing and hazardous. When we have several prescribing doctors, it is vital that adult children and our primary doctor know about all the medications and supplements we are taking. Misuse of medication causes many hospital admissions. (See Exhibit F on pages 218–219.)

As we decline, an adult child may need to fill our pill dispenser and increase supervision of our medications. Jim's father had a stroke after taking twice the amount of an anticoagulant that he was supposed to be taking. Jim regrets not paying more attention to his father's medication. His father—until then, quite alert and competent—overdosed because he was confused after the prescription was changed. The new medication was not only a different color but also a different strength.

Exercise

When we follow a daily exercise program, we will likely stay healthier longer. The plan should include a year-round schedule with alternatives for bad weather. Although there are many good forms of exercise, including swimming and working out at a gym, walking may be preferred because it is easy and inexpensive, and we can do it in our own neighborhoods. We are more likely to continue with walking if our spouse or a friend accompanies us. Some of us prefer walking with our family dog, whose urge to get outside is an extra motivation.

Regular exercise helps us maintain our mobility, assists with balance, and increases muscle strength. There is clear evidence that exercise helps maintain brain health. A study by the University of Illinois showed that three vigorous walks per week over a six-month period increased memory and reasoning ability.[4] It is believed that the brain benefits from the increasing blood flow. In addition, exercise contributes to the health of our bones and helps control blood sugar levels and cholesterol. It can also be a great mood booster. Our adult children can be our partners and play a vital role in assuring that we continue exercising.

Weight control

It is estimated that seventy percent of seniors are overweight. An Oxford University study showed that even moderately obese people are fifty percent more likely to die prematurely.[5] Obesity contributes to developing type 2 diabetes, which has doubled in the senior population over the past fifteen years.

One of the contributors to obesity is the diet that many Americans consume today. Restaurant food, prepackaged meals, and snack foods tend to be high in fat and calories. We live in a culture that encourages overeating. All-you-can-eat buffets are often the choice for seniors when they eat out. Portion sizes everywhere have increased. The plate sizes have increased to accommodate our appetites. Some plates are now so large that they won't fit in our dishwashers. This increase in calories is happening as we are becoming less physically active. Motorized wheelchairs occupied by obese people are becoming common in public places.

Our adult children have a vested interest in keeping us well. It will make their job easier later on. If we have a tendency to overeat and not get enough exercise, they may need to remind us of the consequences, including the likelihood that we won't be able to be active with our grandchildren or attend some family events. Uncontrolled diabetes may contribute to losing vision and, thus, our ability to drive. These reminders may work better than scolding us.

Sleep

Maintaining good sleep is important for keeping us well. As we age, sleep problems can increase from causes such as gastric reflux, pain, or depression. The resulting lack of sleep contributes to hypertension, mental confusion, depression, and excessive anxiety. Insomnia can make us less safe as drivers and can interfere with our social relationships.

Sometimes insomnia comes from sleep apnea—a condition in which the airways are partially blocked. Persons with sleep apnea typically have hundreds of semi-awakenings every night, leading to poor sleep patterns. Snoring is often indicative of sleep apnea, but it is often ignored and seen as a mere annoyance. It may be important to be evaluated at a sleep clinic. If we have sleep apnea, the doctor will recommend a CPAP machine, an air pump attached to a mask that assists with our breathing. Some people resist using one because they have trouble getting used to the mask. But most make the adjustment after a period of time. The longer the sleep apnea condition continues, the more likely it is that serious medical problems will develop.

Practicing good sleep hygiene is important to good sleep. We should sleep approximately eight hours per night. We should avoid caffeine products and alcohol late in the day, and we should refrain from overly stimulating entertainment or conversations before bedtime. It is best to maintain a similar time each night for going to bed and to avoid prolonged or repeated naps during the day.

Mental health

Some of us become depressed or anxious after we retire. While that may come from physical changes within our bodies—including hormonal and circulatory declines—many of the causes are from the changes in our daily routines. Retirement often brings less structure, and many of us lose a sense of purpose and identity. We can be affected by our reduced sense of independence and by financial worries and concerns about health. It is important to talk about our concerns with our spouse and adult children, friends, pastor, or a professional counselor. Our family doctor can also be helpful, especially in prescribing medications that can modify our moods.

To maintain good mental health, we need to discover new activities or hobbies and establish a routine that brings meaningful structure back into our lives. Giving to others through volunteering may be the best medicine of all. Exercise is vital to maintaining good mental health. These new activities can give us a reason to get up in the morning.

Accidents

During our senior years, accidents can happen in many ways. One of the most common is from falls. More than a third of seniors experience a fall that causes an injury. Falls are a leading reason for hospital admissions.[6] Changes in balance, vision, and reduced strength increase the risk of an accident. Few of us make accurate assessments of our abilities and of the risks involved. We need our adult children to coach us when it comes to safety. They may see things that we don't.

We can reduce our risks by developing a healthy respect for height. We should avoid ladders and refrain from climbing trees. We need to be especially careful on stairways and icy sidewalks and give special attention to uneven surfaces. Our adult children can help us do a safety audit of our home. Some of the changes they may suggest include rearranging the furniture to avoid tripping over chair legs, removing loose rugs, adding grab bars in the bathroom, and improving lighting.

One of our most significant safety risks—and most difficult to discuss—comes from driving. Seniors have an at-fault accident record that is second only to teen drivers.[7] To remain safe drivers we should:

- Drive more slowly.

- Allow more distance between our car and the car in front of us.

- Enter highways only where there are stoplights, as much as possible.

- Avoid crossing two lanes when entering a highway, which involves traffic coming from two directions.

- Stay away from hazardous intersections.

- Drive when traffic volume is lower.

- Not drive after dark or when we are tired.

- Avoid distractions from cell phones, interruptions from passengers, changing radio stations, or adjusting the fan.

Soon after retirement, we should put in writing criteria to determine when we should give up driving. (See Exhibit G on pages 220–221.) A checklist can be an objective way to measure our safety on the road. AARP, AAA, and some insurance companies provide helpful information. AAA and AARP conduct a safe driving school for seniors. Hopefully we will recognize the decline ourselves and voluntarily give up driving if we are at risk.

But many of us won't recognize when our driving has become unsafe. An early agreement with our adult children gives them the freedom to ask for our keys and to sell our vehicle. This loss of independence is not easy and can have profound effects on all of us. Partnering with our adult children to plan for alternative transportation is essential. It is important to recognize that our safety—and the safety of others—is at stake.

When Joe talked with his mother in her late eighties about no longer driving, she was relieved to be free of the responsibility. She said, "My children listened to me when they were young, and now I want to listen to them." The older we are when we start these discussions, the more difficult they may be for many of us.

Sue moved to Portland to be near her sons when she was in her seventies. She chose to live where she had easy access to public transportation and sold her car.

She usually calls friends if she needs a ride to places not accessed by public transit. Occasionally her sons drive her. She is relieved not to drive in the city.

Dental health

We have known for many years that good dental health contributes to a longer and higher quality of life. Recent studies connect gum disease as a contributing factor to heart disease, diabetes, dementia, and other chronic illnesses. Loss of teeth prevents proper chewing of food, which in turn can create a choking hazard and prolonged digestion. Food that is not chewed adequately is more difficult to digest and increases gastric reflux and delayed digestion.

Adult children can make sure we receive regular dental care. Providing our transportation to the dentist allows them to form a partnership with our dentist, making good treatment decisions smoother. Because many of us are reluctant to spend money on dental care, adult children play a key role in making sure that finances are available for adequate care. They may even be able to work with our dentist to develop a payment plan or assist with the cost. This partnership will improve our dental care decisions and decrease the incidence of disease.

Early decline in health

In spite of all the prevention steps that we take, our bodies will decline. For many of us, the decline will be minor at first and won't seriously affect our quality of life. One of the most common health problems that we experience during our senior years is hearing loss. This happens to about two-thirds of us before we may be fully aware of it.[8] Often our adult children approach us about our hearing loss, but we minimize the problem. Or we may deny that they have said anything about it. (Maybe we didn't hear them!) We often blame others for not speaking loudly enough. Even though our hearing loss makes social interactions more difficult, we resist getting hearing aids. We say they are uncomfortable to wear, hard to adjust, and much too expensive. Vanity may be the biggest reason. Hearing is an important way to stay connected to those around us.

Eye health

Our eyes may also be a cause for concern. Although many of us have worn glasses for a long time, some changes now are more troubling. We may need to have cataracts removed. We might develop macular degeneration, glaucoma, detached retinas, or other serious eye diseases. Poor vision can cause us to lose our drivers' licenses, make us more susceptible to falls, and make reading difficult. Improved surgical procedures and other advances can treat these conditions, but we may lose our vision simply because we resist making a doctor's appointment.

Conditions like diabetes, hypertension, and arthritis can worsen as we age. Because our body systems are weakening, we may need to take insulin to bring our diabetes under control or increase our hypertension medication. Medication to control our arthritis may become less effective, and pain may be a more constant companion. We become aware that more peers are having joint replacement surgery.

Sometimes a medical crisis comes to us by surprise. While visiting his daughter in California, John, then sixty-five and recently retired, suffered a heart attack and needed emergency surgery to save his life. He had none of the markers of heart disease. John feels like he has been given a second chance. He and his wife, Sally, experience each new day as a gift.

By contrast, Sue became aware of her heart problems more gradually. She knew that something was wrong when she could no longer climb steps without stopping several times. Her doctor confirmed the presence of heart disease and prescribed medication. Sue also made lifestyle changes to improve her health.

Some of us will be diagnosed with cancer. When it arrives, we are filled with fear and the dread of treatment. We don't look forward to invasive surgery, chemotherapy, or radiation. Even though some forms of this disease have good survival rates, others do not. Whatever our particular cancer may be, it will likely change our lives in a major way.

When these changes in our health take place, it becomes even more important that our adult children accompany us to doctor visits. Their more objective presence helps us make the best decisions about treatment. They will ask questions we hadn't thought of and hear some details we miss. We can review together what we all heard from the doctor. Most of all, they provide emotional support during stressful times of treatment.

When Lloyd's mother developed dementia, he and his wife, Mim, wanted to be involved by giving direct care and supporting his father. At that time, Lloyd's parents were living in another state. Active involvement in her medical care meant talking regularly with doctors, going with her to appointments, monitoring medications, and being involved in decision-making about her future. They knew that couldn't happen if his parents remained in their home.

Lloyd renovated his and Mim's house, converting the dining room into a bedroom. He updated a bathroom nearby to make it wheelchair-accessible and added safety bars by the commode and tub. After Lloyd's parents are gone, he'll remove the temporary wall that formed the bedroom, converting it back to a dining room.

Lloyd and Mim have become an active part of his parents' medical team. Their children support the caregiving when they can and benefit from interaction with their grandparents.

Life at the end: hard choices

Unless we die suddenly, the decline in our health will increase in severity and complexity. We will need our family even more, and the earlier conversations we have had with our adult children will be helpful. It is difficult to know what to do when an illness has no remedy or when treatments carry a high risk. Our age, level of cognitive functioning, and the presence of other complicating conditions factor into our health decisions.

If we are diagnosed with prostate cancer when we are eighty-five, should we proceed with treatment that produces ongoing side effects? When an orthopedist suggests surgery for an arthritic spine when we are sixty-eight but can't promise to completely resolve our pain, what should we do? If we are in our nineties and the cardiologist recommends a pacemaker, should we proceed if we are showing signs of dementia? Do we want to live to be one hundred even if we aren't aware of our surroundings?

Our adult children should be with us during doctor visits to be sure we are gathering enough information. Understanding the recovery possibilities and how the treatment will affect our quality of life are important considerations. Adult children need to be our partners in decision-making.

Mahlon developed an aggressive form of pseudobulbar palsy in his sixties and gradually lost his ability to care for himself. As the condition worsened, he had difficulty swallowing. The doctor recommended a feeding tube to provide proper nutrition. Mahlon said no to that idea. The medical staff asked him three different times until they were satisfied with his answer. His wife, Esther, and their children were at peace with the decision not to extend his life in this way. He had minimal quality of life, and death was a release for him. It was still a painful loss. Mahlon died at the age of seventy.

When my (Gerald's) mother—then one hundred years old—fell and experienced bleeding in her brain, the doctor wanted to operate to relieve the pressure. She was competent enough to refuse and was returned to the nursing home where she had been living. A week later, she had further bleeding and lost her ability to speak. This time she could only shake her head "no" when the medical staff wanted to return her to the hospital for treatment. She was able to write her wishes: "I want to die. I am ready to die." My siblings who were present felt some pressure from the staff to override her wishes. They asked, "Why wouldn't you want your mother to have the procedure? She might be able to speak again." The family was in complete agreement with our mother to refuse further treatment. She was transferred to a hospice center and died peacefully a week later.

Truman was seventy-nine years old and in serious decline from atypical Parkinson's disease when he developed meningitis and was hospitalized. When he didn't respond to the treatment, the attending doctor suggested he be flown to a teaching hospital across the mountains for more aggressive care. His wife, Betty, and their adult children were concerned about the quality of life for Truman and knew the experimental treatment was not what he would have wanted. Betty told the doctor, "This is one trip over the mountain that Truman will not have to make." He died peacefully several days later in the hospital.

Despite the fact that most of us say we want to die at home, eighty percent of us die in a hospital.[9] It is where we usually go when we are sick or injured. We tend to seek care in hospitals even when it is clear that we have little chance of recovery. In the view of Daniel Callahan and Sherwin Nuland of the Hastings Center, too much of health care today consists of ways to "marginally extend the lives of the very sick."

In more recent years, many of the very sick have begun to choose a hospice center as the place where they want to die. Some of us die at home while being attended to by hospice workers. The ability of hospice to offer palliative care to the dying and to give emotional support to relatives is unmatched. Helping us accept death as a normal part of living can be invaluable. Callahan writes about a social solidarity model that emphasizes "caring as much as curing."

Dr. Glenn Stoltzfus says that in his experience from working in a hospital, the family must be united in supporting the end-of-life wishes when their loved one is hospitalized in critical condition. He cautions that any papers that have been prepared are "only conversation starters" and mean little unless all family members support the wish not to extend treatment. Otherwise, doctors will continue to offer life-extending procedures, which is their mandate as physicians.

Dr. David J. Casarett, a palliative care physician and researcher, suggests that when we have a life-threatening illness or injury, we must discuss our wishes for our remaining time with family members and physicians. The decisions we make can create an atmosphere that will give all of us more control, a greater sense of peace, and dignity. He suggests that each of us answer the following questions:

- Where do we want to be when we die?

- With whom do we want to spend our remaining time?

- How do we want to spend the time that we are given?

- Are there any unsettled issues with family and friends that we want to resolve?

- How do we want to die?

Facing the end of life is never easy. Although we and our family may feel a great deal of sadness about the loss that is coming, we want that time to be as meaningful as possible. While none of us can prevent our deaths, many of us can shape the way we die.

Ending thoughts

Although there is much that we can do to stay well and safe throughout our senior years, the end of life is certain. We *will* decline, and we *will* die. In the meantime, we are embedded in a culture that finds new ways to improve the quality and length of life. While we are still well, we need to be good stewards of our health by choosing a lifestyle of wellness. We need to be passionate about making the kinds of choices that help keep us as well as possible. We do that because it is good for our family, for us, and our society. Unnecessary medical expenses are a burden on everyone.

When our health declines, we need the help of our adult children to determine what the next steps should be, especially about appropriate treatment for life-threatening illnesses.

At some point, the severity of our decline will limit the effectiveness of treatments. It will be difficult to know when to say no to further treatment. The conversations that began earlier will help us make these decisions with more certainty. Our commitment to the stewardship of our resources—and those of the broader society—can influence us to avoid high-risk medical interventions that promise limited improvement. Many times, they can intrude on the natural process of dying.

Maybe we can say, as Earl did when cancer had spread through his body, "I've lived seventy-nine good years, and I'm ready to die." He declined further treatment and left this life peacefully in his home, surrounded by his family. He practiced what many people would consider good stewardship. His widow and family are also at peace. When we die we all leave behind a legacy that includes our end-of-life decisions.

Questions

1. At what point should adult children talk with their parents about preventive lifestyle changes?

2. As parents' health declines, when should adult children ask to go along with them to doctors' appointments?

3. What keeps parents from talking openly with their adult children about health?

4. What can be done if adult children and their parents aren't able to talk about end-of-life issues?

CHAPTER 8

Left Behind

ONE EXPERIENCE: *I don't know whether it makes any difference if I visit my husband in the nursing home every day. He's so confused that I don't think he even recognizes me. In some ways it seems like he has already died. He was diagnosed with Alzheimer's a few years ago, but I saw him slipping away long before that. It's so hard to see him in this condition. We had forty very good years. He was bright and outgoing—and now this. But we made a sacred promise to each other, and I will do what I can to be with him to the end. I still love him—maybe now more than ever.*

ANOTHER EXPERIENCE: *When my wife died a year ago, I didn't know how hard it would be. We had no time to prepare for what happened. Neither of us knew that she had a heart condition, and her death took even the doctor by surprise. Now I wish we had talked about dying. There's so much I should have told her, and so much we could have done. But she was only sixty and seemed to be in good health. We took too much for granted. Now I have a hard time sleeping. I've lost twenty pounds. I know I'm only sixty-two and could get married again. But I can't bear the thought. My kids are telling me that I have to get out more, and they even hint that I should soon start dating. But not now—maybe never.*

Early in our marriages, we tend not to think about losing our spouses to death or disabling disease. Now we can't escape these thoughts when we attend funerals or try to comfort friends whose spouses are in nursing homes. None of us can ignore the despair we see in their eyes. We begin to realize that it could happen to us. It is a reality that has now become a part of our lives.

Maybe that's why each of us is more aware of the chest pains or memory lapses in our spouses. For a time we are reassured by negative tests. But thoughts of life without our spouses—the grief and the loneliness—become more common. We imagine what it would be like to attend events by ourselves, to eat alone, and to no longer share our inner thoughts. We have little experience with aloneness and don't look forward to it.

Our adult children are also confronted with thoughts of losing us. Although the implications are different for them, our deaths or illnesses will change their lives as well. They may need to support us, and connections between a surviving parent and adult children become especially important.

Left behind by chronic illness

Spouses can feel left behind when a husband or wife is incapacitated. Elvin was diagnosed with multiple sclerosis when he was thirty-three years old. He and Roberta had been married eight years when he began showing symptoms. She felt keenly the responsibility of raising their two young children alone, especially as the disease left him unable to communicate and confined to a wheelchair. During those years she gave him wonderful care and unlimited love. Friends and family gave her some assistance. As the illness progressed Roberta was, in some ways, a widow.

A similar feeling of abandonment can come when a spouse develops dementia. Early-onset Alzheimer's disease, a disabling brain condition that can show symptoms in one's fifties, is particularly troubling. We experience profound grief knowing that our loved ones are beginning to lose their ability to reason, remember, and relate to us. The body is alive but not the mind. As a couple, we had been looking forward to many good years together in retirement. Now those dreams are shattered. Alzheimer's disease and other forms of dementia affect about one in three families. Some studies suggest that the incidence of Alzheimer's will increase by twenty percent within twenty years.[1]

More common forms of dementia typically appear later in life. Though the patients are older, families still feel helpless and sad when a loved one changes into a different person. Seth began showing signs of forgetfulness when he was in his late seventies. This highly skilled craftsman had high standards for the cabinets and furniture he built. He was also diligent about finances and his checkbook. As his illness progressed, Seth found it more difficult to craft furniture to his satisfaction. He had trouble balancing his checkbook. At first he blamed the bank for the accounting mistakes. His wife, Ginny, became more concerned when he had trouble handling the money for his class reunion, for which he served as treasurer, something he had done with precision for many years.

Seth was also aware that something was wrong. When he was still alert enough to ask Ginny about his confusion, she suggested that it could be dementia. It was as if he had already known and was relieved to have it acknowledged. His only request to her was, "Will you hang in there with me?"

It was not an easy decision for Ginny to move him from their cottage into skilled care at the continuing care community where they lived. In the four years leading up to his death, he became profoundly incapacitated and was unable to communicate. Although she was occasionally comforted by a smile from Seth, Ginny was left behind by an illness that took her loving husband's spirit away. After his death, Ginny took comfort in knowing that she had kept her promise to "hang in there" throughout his illness.

Although our adult children experience our disabilities differently than we do, they usually affect them deeply. Children must adjust to a changing relationship with the declining parent, and this new reality alters family gatherings. Some may even come to an end.

Adult children who are directly involved in giving care and support to parents during this time can carry a heavy load. Seth and Ginny's adult children were helpful to their mother during their father's decline. They suffered along with their parents.

Left behind by death

For some of us, the death of our spouse happens without warning early in our retirement years. Sometimes it occurs suddenly from an accident or unexpected illness. Because we have no time to prepare, we are left numb and in grief. We survive because of the support of family and friends and from the comfort that faith can bring.

Many of us have more time to prepare for losing a spouse. It may be decline over time from an incurable illness, such as cancer or chronic heart failure. Under those circumstances death may be easier to accept. Sometimes we may even pray for death to come. We might reject lifesaving medical intervention and allow death to follow its normal course. But even these deaths bring a deep sense of loss when we reflect on the good times we had together before the illness began. Gone now is the companionship that we treasured for so many years.

After Edgar's wife, Gladys, died at age eighty, he wrote her the following:

When I woke up on Monday morning (April 12)... no let's go back a few days. Remember? It was Saturday. We loaded our newspapers into the car and headed for Daniel's, your farmer friend. While I unloaded the papers, the children deposited the baby goat on your lap, dirty feet and all. You didn't seem to mind—you always enjoyed the kids. Then we headed across country in the direction of Manheim. We were not sure of the road, but the direction seemed right and we enjoyed the ride. Farmers were working their fields, some with horses. Flowers and blossoming trees were in full bloom; not a cloud in the sky. Temperature—shirtsleeve-comfortable. I commented, "What a nice spring day." You said, "Maybe my last." We wiped a few tears and motored on.

Sunday after lunch I went for a long walk, and when I returned I found a note saying that you had gone to visit Anita, who was recovering from a long illness. I probably watched some TV—you read. Then you remembered some bills that needed to be paid. It did not go well. I was afraid you would resign from tending our family finances, something you had done and done very well for years. After a bit you said, "The rest can wait—I am so tired—and confused."

We went to bed. I gave you the usual back rub. You thanked me and we bade each other a good night. Then you appended, "I love you." I assured you that I loved you, too—and so the day ended, your last at 929 Broad Street.

Gladys suffered a stroke the next morning and died ten days later.

The impact of the death of a parent on adult children will vary, depending on the circumstances. If we are seventy years old when we die, it will probably have a greater impact on our adult children than if we are one hundred. When the death happens suddenly, it is hard for them to prepare for the loss. Often the death means that the adult child will provide a great deal of support to the surviving parent. Seeing his or her emotional pain can add to the grief of an adult child. Many assume this new role willingly and find healing for their grief through helping their parent. When adult children lose both parents, they experience an increased feeling of emptiness and aloneness. The family of origin now exists only in memory and through relationships with siblings.

Preparing for being alone

The best preparation any of us can make for being alone is to maintain relationships that are transparent and have integrity until the end. We don't want to enter our senior years with unsettled conflict—with our spouse or our adult children. We don't want to live—and die—with anything hidden or unresolved. Even though most of us have regrets for things we have said or done throughout our lives, it becomes increasingly important that we deal with these issues early in our senior years. If we develop an illness that impairs our minds, or if we die suddenly, it is too late to apologize, forgive, explain, or to clear up any doubts.

Too many survivors are left behind with "if onlys." It would be tragic to face our ends with unfinished conversations. We must be committed to deal with any unfinished apologies or unoffered forgiveness. If we can't resolve these differences by ourselves, it is important that we seek the help of a pastor or a counselor. In the words of the poet Robert Frost, we have "promises to keep and miles to go before we sleep." One of those promises is to be at peace with each other before we sleep.

Kal and Edna were interviewed by the Portland *Oregonian* around Valentine's Day, just as they were celebrating seventy-four years of marriage. When they were asked what kept them together all those years, Edna replied, "We had our differences, but I can't remember what any of them were!" Kal said, "It took me too many years to say I'm sorry first."

Early family conversations about our deaths

As hard as it may be, it is very important for families to prepare early for what is coming. Start the conversation about death even though it might seem remote at that time. Approach the subject as a natural part of life—not a separate event. Set aside any aversion to talking openly about it—even if the grandchildren might hear what we are saying. Just like parents and adult children need to prepare for aging, we also need to prepare for dying. There may be nothing else in our lives for which we need to be more prepared.

Planning our funerals

We should talk with our adult children about our funeral services. (See Exhibit H on pages 222–223.) It is helpful for each of us to list favorite Scriptures, songs, and poems, and identify who should lead the service and who should participate otherwise. Obviously, if we live for a long time, those choices may need to be changed. We may outlive ministers or others whom we want to conduct and include in the funeral.

These funeral plans are a guide and should not restrict the thoughts and feelings of the adult children or surviving parent. This may be the first time the children are stepping into a position of leadership with their surviving parent.

Most family members want people who have been important to them to offer eulogies. Their remarks should be modest, honest, and respectful. They should avoid hyperbole that tries to deflect our grief. We can anticipate that the funeral will be a time of sadness, as well as a time of reflecting on positive memories of our loved one.

In many faith communities, the service is a spiritual experience, recognizing that death brings us to the threshold of the eternal and the infinite. Even though some faiths may refer to golden streets and palaces in the next life, the service also needs to help the bereaved accept the mystery that is connected with death. Many faiths express the hope of a renewed life. That belief allows the family to face their loss with an assurance that death is a beginning and not just an end.

Families need to make many decisions in the midst of grief. The choices for how to dispose of the body have become more varied in recent years. Many families want an alternative to an expensive casket and large displays of flowers. Some churches now make simple wooden caskets available for their members, reflecting a spirit of simplicity and ecological sensitivity. Families have found the experience of making a casket together to be a healing time. Religious groups like the Quakers have been preparing the body and privately burying their deceased for five hundred years. The Amish and some plain Mennonite groups have long traditions of simple funerals and burials that include hand-built coffins.

A growing percentage of us now choose cremation,[2] after which the remains are buried or scattered, depending on the preferences of the family. Family members may have differing views about cremation, based on religious convictions or personal preferences. Some persons believe that there is value in having close relatives—including grandchildren—be able to view the body of the deceased prior to burial or cremation.[3] Sometimes families gather at the bedside at the time of death to say their good-byes. Others choose to donate their bodies to medical science. John was surprised when his mother—then ninety-one—wanted to talk with him about doing just that. She was not feeling good about spending a lot of money for her funeral but wanted to do something that might help other people.

In his book *Accompany Them with Singing*,[4] author Thomas Long suggests that we reclaim the funeral as a sacramental event—similar in many ways to baptism and communion. He believes that the body should be present at the funeral, even in cremated form. As an act of love for the deceased and in support of the family, the community can then accompany the body to its final resting place. He laments the fact that many families choose to dispose of the body before the funeral, making it the only important religious event of our lives—such as baptism, communion, or a wedding—for which the body is not present.

Increasingly, funerals are referred to as a "memorial service" or a "celebration of life." Could this euphemistic language be an attempt to minimize our loss and grief? Perhaps we are more comfortable with celebrations and want to quickly return to our normal lives. Of course, a respectful amount of remembering and honoring the life of the deceased is appropriate and a source of comfort to the family.

Grieving

Moments of humor can lighten grief, but humor should not be used to cover feelings of loss. The human spirit needs to cry and grieve. To say that a funeral brings closure suggests a clinical fantasy more than reality. The idea that the family will neatly find its way through the various "stages of grief" seems offensive. Those theories may work in a textbook but not usually in the real world.

With such a great diversity of human experience, it is simplistic to suggest that everyone will follow the same grieving script. When a parent has been ill for a long time, the family has already grieved and may even feel a sense of relief when their loved one dies. Greg and his siblings expressed just that at their father's funeral. They reflected on having lost their father some ten years earlier when his dementia robbed him of his ability to relate to them. Now they were free to reflect on some of their good memories of their father.

New realities after the funeral

In the weeks and months following the funeral, the surviving spouse and adult children are faced with new realities. Hopefully, these realities had been a part of earlier discussions with the deceased spouse and the adult children. Ideally, the plan includes details about finances and the possible variables the survivors may face. Will the surviving spouse have enough money to live on as a single person? Is s/he competent to pay bills, balance the checkbook, and handle other financial details? If not, the family needs to find a skillful and trustworthy person to manage this.

Another reality to face is where the surviving parent will live. S/he may decide to stay where s/he is if her/his health is good. Losing a spouse and a home at the same time can be difficult. Depending on the circumstances, it can be helpful to have an adult child stay with the parent during the night for awhile. Some survivors occasionally take in boarders to provide some income and support.

The surviving spouse should be prepared to move if it is not safe to live alone or if s/he can't afford the upkeep. The move may be to a smaller house or apartment, to a retirement community, or to live with one of the adult children. Having had earlier conversations with them about these options can make decisions easier now.

The spouse who wants to live independently should be able to handle daily living needs. Does s/he know how to cook, clean, do laundry, manage the property, and care for the car and personal health? Although a parent can get some support from adult children or from others for these tasks—especially during the early to middle senior years—having these skills is essential for maintaining independence. If parents allow themselves to become dependent on others prematurely, they will likely experience earlier aging and reduced quality of life, and need institutional care earlier.

After the death of a spouse, the survivor begins a new social life, now as an individual. S/he is no longer a wife or husband. The survivor's identity becomes very personal. Although the parent will turn to adult children for advice, in many cases ultimate decision-making now rests on her or his shoulders. The relationships formed during marriage tended to be with other couples; now the survivor is an individual in a couple's world.

It's important to develop new personal interests—perhaps by volunteering or joining new groups. If the survivor is living in a retirement community, it may be easier to develop a social life. Adult children can play a role in providing companionship, but they can't be a permanent replacement for friendships and social activities. It's not fair to them, and it can also limit the survivor's involvement with others.

Remarriage

Although most survivors remain single, some do remarry. Remarriage should always be discussed with adult children. It is even more important the older the parent is. If adult children suspect that their parent isn't fully competent, they may need to convince her or him that the marriage is not appropriate.

The following points are important to think about before considering remarriage:

- The survivor's age and the age of the potential spouse.

- How soon after the death of the original spouse the survivor began dating.

- The survivor's emotional and physical health and that of the potential spouse.

- Religious and cultural differences.

- The relationship between adult children and potential step-parent.

- Financial arrangements.

When Richard's father, then in his late eighties, announced that he was going to marry for the third time, Richard and his siblings were very concerned. He hadn't done well in his first marriage when he was married to their mother. His second marriage lasted fifty years because, in Richard's words, "she stood her ground" on many of their decisions. He was domineering with both his wives.

When he told his children of his intention to marry a third time, he assured them that he and his wife-to-be had met with a lawyer and signed a prenuptial agreement. He said that the family would not have to worry about the finances. They soon discovered that his plan was to take care of his new wife. This became evident as he continued to use money in controlling and manipulative ways with other family members. Richard's third marriage lasted ten years. After his death, his widow changed the will and bequeathed all of the inheritance to her only son, from whom she had been estranged. Richard and his siblings were left only with the responsibility of disposing of the contents of their father's home.

It is vital that the parent and adult children talk together about remarriage. No one wants the surviving spouse to make an impulsive decision based on loneliness or dependency. Emotions may lead parents into a short courtship. They may rationalize that they are making the right decision because of their mature age and life experience. Hopefully, the surviving parent and adult children are committed to making this decision slowly and carefully.

While remarriage can be rich and meaningful—and sometimes even better than one's original marriage—it can also be complicated. It usually brings with it separate sets of adult children and grandchildren, plus family histories and rituals that are quite varied. These differences are at times hard to adjust to. It can be a challenge to know how to honor the memory of an original spouse, while at the same time giving full love and commitment to the new spouse. Problems can also arise if one spouse brings a very different financial situation, including debt, into a marriage. Or one spouse may bring greater financial assets into the marriage than the other spouse does. A prenuptial agreement can ensure that all adult children are treated fairly.

Many people find a fresh purpose in their new relationship, one that is life-giving—sometimes literally bringing physical, emotional, and spiritual health. This may happen most keenly after caring a long time for a sick spouse. The new relationship can allow a couple to become active and reengaged with life. If it is a compatible marriage, the adult children and grandchildren can celebrate the new union and may even feel less responsibility to support their parent.

Mike and Karen entered their second marriage when they were in their mid-sixties. Mike had lost his first wife after a long battle with cancer. They had had a close relationship through forty-three years of marriage. They had lived in a number of different communities because Mike was a pastor. His wife was very supportive of him. When she was first diagnosed with cancer, she and Mike were optimistic about her chance of recovery. After some recurrences, it became clear that she would not live. They grieved deeply in the months leading up to her death. Their four children and several young grandchildren also were deeply affected by her death.

Karen's husband, a college professor, was killed instantly in a car accident when she was fifty-nine. Even though they loved each other, they were both busy with their careers and didn't talk much together—especially about the future. Karen was not prepared for this moment. Her grief was great, but the shock was even greater. As a relatively young widow, she was left to deal with details that she found overwhelming. Their two young adult children were just establishing their own homes in other states and were also deeply affected by the tragedy.

Mike and Karen and their families had known each other for many years before their spouses died. Since Karen's husband had died some years earlier, she sent condolences to Mike when she heard of his wife's death. That contact eventually opened the door to a new friendship. They soon talked with their children about their budding relationship.

Although the adult children had no wish to blend together, they all supported the new marriage. The families celebrate holidays separately, partly because of the complexities in the number of persons involved and possibly to maintain some identity with their deceased parent. The grandchildren find it natural to relate to their new grandparents since they are the only ones that they have known.

Mike and Karen find it easy to have open communication with each other and often talk about the future. They feel comforted that they are able to talk about their previous spouses with each other and with their children. That preserves their memories, while at the same time giving them freedom to celebrate their new life together.

Matt and Sue were in a happy marriage for many years when Sue was diagnosed with a life-threatening illness in her late sixties. They both knew that she would not live long. They had a close relationship and a tight-knit family that included adult children and grandchildren. The family made the decision to care for Sue at home. Matt was supported by many caregivers from their church and community, which allowed the family to spend time together during her decline and the freedom to grieve in their own ways. They occasionally talked about her approaching death. After Sue died, Matt was deeply touched by notes from Sue that he found for himself, the children, and the grandchildren. They were to be read on Christmas Day, and she released him to move on with his life.

After many years of a happy marriage, Beth faced the loss of her husband Tony more suddenly. He suffered a severe stroke in his late fifties and died three days later. Because of previous health problems, Tony sensed that his life might be shortened by his illnesses. He told her, "When I die, I may die quickly." Beth and Tony had talked some about his potential early death, but it was difficult for Beth to discuss it openly. However, the brief talks prepared her for his death, and she now sees his words as a gift to her.

After both of their spouses died, Matt and Beth supported each other through occasional phone calls. They had known each other for many years. Their families had been good friends and shared some special occasions together. Eventually, the contacts became more frequent, and they formed a special bond, to their surprise.

When Matt talked with his children about marrying Beth, they expressed appreciation for his desire to have their support and blessing. The grandchildren were excited about Matt getting married. Beth's grandchildren were born after Tony's death. When she told them she was getting married, the grandchildren had questions about what would it be like to have a grandpa. Her adult children were supportive of the marriage. The two families do not get together often since the adult children live in different communities.

Matt and Beth signed a prenuptial agreement to ensure fair distribution of assets to their adult children. They talk with each other as opportunities, changes, and choices emerge, aiding in their various decision-making processes.

Ending thoughts

We all know that some day we may lose our spouse—either to death or to a significant disability. It is especially important to face that reality at the beginning of our senior years. Statistics compel us to talk together about the inevitable. The discussion doesn't need to be morbid or create an unnecessary sense of gloom. We do each other a favor, too, by talking with our adult children about what is eventually coming. We should discuss various possibilities that typically occur as we age—especially severe disability and death—and how our adult children can be helpful during that time.

None of us can ever fully prepare for the loss, grief, and helplessness we experience when a spouse or parent becomes disabled or dies. Talking about it earlier may have helped us face the loss with more clarity, but the emotions that sweep over us can still be wrenching. As spouses and adult children, we really are left behind. Although we have friends and may find comfort from our faith, we need others to provide support during this time of emptiness. We carry the burden together, and we heal together. Life can go on. We can find our way to a new place. The partnership that we formed with our adult children is now more important than ever.

Questions

1. How is a living death from a long-term illness different from a final death?

2. If adult children or their parents aren't able to talk about end-of-life issues, what might be done to help overcome their resistance?

3. If there is a difference of opinion regarding the funeral and disposition of the body, how can a family work to resolve these differences?

4. How can family members find new life together after the death of their loved one?

CHAPTER 9

A Legacy of Family Conversations

The choices we make during our senior years shape our legacy. They demonstrate stewardship of resources—both ours and the broader society's. They also send messages about the importance of family, shared decision-making, and the need to plan wisely for the future. Perhaps most importantly, our choices reflect our character. How honest and open are we in our conversations? How willing are we to give to others instead of expecting to receive? Do we accept support from our children with grace? Hopefully we engage them in positive ways, which they will pass on to their children and to others whose lives they touch.

The following stories are about legacy. They illustrate how families work together in preparing for the parents' later years. Some stories are understated; the storytellers were concerned that they not sound boastful. But all the families shared their stories to encourage others to talk openly about aging. No single plan works for every family. But when families plan for the future together—and carry out that plan—they usually achieve a better end.

Co-author Gerald Kaufman: A thirty-five-year conversation

My father died at age sixty-eight of black lung disease and heart failure. My mother was sixty-five and living in Johnstown, Pennsylvania, where I had been born. I was living in the eastern part of the state, a three-hour drive away. My sisters lived within walking distance, "just up the hollow," from our mother. One of my brothers was a ten-minute drive away, and my oldest brother lived in the Midwest.

Our mother had been highly dependent on my father and only learned to drive in her fifties. After he died, she struggled not only with her grief but with living alone. Much of the responsibility for helping her cope fell on the shoulders of my siblings who lived nearby. They got some relief for several years when a young male teacher came to board in her home. She enjoyed cooking for him and liked not being alone.

When he married and moved out several years later, my mother decided to move into a mobile home close to one of my sisters. That arrangement worked well until some health crises developed. My sister was the person she called—sometimes during the night. Several times my mother ended up in the emergency room.

It became clear that living alone was no longer possible. We siblings scheduled a meeting to talk about moving her to a nearby nursing care facility. When she learned of the meeting, she asked to join us, saying, "It's about me, and I should be a part of it." She wanted the conversation, which should have happened much earlier. By the end of the meeting, we all agreed that now was the time for the move. At ninety-one, she became a resident in the assisted living section. Her adjustment was made easier by the presence of a lifelong friend who lived in the next room. Once our mother was comfortable, my local siblings could live more normal lives again.

My brother and his wife in the Midwest began visiting her during their annual trip to our home community. They took her on car rides, reminisced about ancestors and family trips to Oregon, and brought her up to date about their grandchildren. Throughout the rest of the year, they called on Sunday evenings and wrote to her regularly. They sent money for her personal spending account, allowing her to buy things that were important to her.

Because Marlene and I lived closer, we were able to make more frequent visits to see her. We took her to a small country store where she could get some bargains and to pick elderberries where she had picked them when she was younger. We walked across a long swinging bridge that brought back memories from her youth. She hung on carefully while watching the rushing river beneath her feet. When she got back on land, it took her a while to regain her balance. She especially counted on us taking her to a nearby steakhouse. She said the food was better there than in the dining hall. Institutional food was a challenge for her. We also phoned regularly and contributed money for her personal spending account.

As she became weaker and less steady on her feet, she wasn't able to enjoy her surroundings as much. Her sight and hearing were diminishing. She lost many of her friends to death or senility. Life was fading, and its meaning was disappearing. But her mind remained alert, which made it discouraging for her to be among residents who were quite limited. She attended activities but was often the only resident who knew the answers to the game questions. That made it more important than ever that she had family members to talk with.

Because of her decline, my sisters visited more often and talked frequently with her by phone. My local brother had moved to another state but continued to manage her finances. He returned frequently to the community and stopped in to see her. When she reached her one-hundredth birthday, family and friends planned a celebration for her. Less than a year later, she suffered a brain injury from a fall and died in hospice care several days later. To the end she was surrounded by family and still conversing—using written notes when she lost her ability to speak. For her, the various stages of her senior years called for new solutions that were worked out with her family.

The Zimmerman family: Conversations through actions

Jonathan and Ada, members of the Old Order Mennonite church, welcomed us (the authors) warmly into their simple apartment. It is attached to the main house where their son, daughter-in-law, and eight grandchildren live. In their church community, it is common for extended families to live near each other. Even though five of Jonathan and Ada's adult children have moved to different states in search of more affordable land, three remain in the home community.

Soon after we had settled into our chairs in the Martins' home, their grandchildren began to enter the room. They quietly took seats and listened carefully to what was being said. Later their mother joined us, carrying a newborn child. One of the grandchildren was sent outside to find out when the father and sixteen-year-old brother would be coming in from the barn.

It is obvious that this family is committed to remaining tightly connected to each other in the cycle from birth to death. Although members of this faith tradition tend to converse more with actions than with words, when they do speak, their words carry importance. Their traditions help their faith and their way of living to be passed on. Because of the strong family and church connections, they depend little on government agencies to provide care for their elderly. They talk relatively little about the changes that come with aging. Their traditions and ways of living are a kind of conversation.

Their commitments are also seen in the ways they share their compassion with others who aren't a part of their church. Ada's parents offered significant care to an "English" neighbor when she developed a terminal illness. Later, when Ada's parents moved to a new community, the neighbor's husband, then a widower, asked to move along with them. He lived in a trailer behind their house and ate his meals with them. They cared for him until his death. As Ada was telling this story, the grandchildren paid close attention. Clearly the idea of caring for family, and for neighbors, was being imprinted on their young minds.

Jeff and Margaret Smith: Giving as conversation

Jeff and Margaret are retired professionals in their sixties and active doing short-term volunteer assignments. Jeff sold his share of his business at age sixty, something he'd begun planning in his forties. Jeff and Margaret had careers independent from each other and looked forward to finding ways to work together in their retirement years, as God gave them strength and health.

When looking at their retirement, Jeff and Margaret set some goals for travel and service. These goals would be difficult to meet if they continued to live in their large home. Realizing this, they chose to downsize and to move to a condominium community. They were able to pass on the family "stuff." It was rewarding to see their adult children and grandchildren enjoy these things and put them to practical use.

Some advantages of condo living for Jeff and Margaret include the freedom to help others, whether it is their children, community, or through church-related service projects. This freedom also makes it more possible to travel. In addition, they find they enjoy the community life that condo living provides.

They are passionate about reaching out to those around them who may not have family support. One way they've done this is by purchasing a rental property for a single friend with no immediate family. It is a pattern they learned from the generation before them and are gratified to see their children doing some of the same things. Jeff's and Margaret's actions are an important part of the conversation they have with their family. And they have a broader view of who is family.

Jeff helped his widowed mother to make many decisions as she approached a decline in her health. Decisions about where to live and when to stop driving are easier when discussed and decided before they are absolutely necessary.

Jeff and Margaret laugh when they remember how they wrestled with the decision to downsize. They worried whether family time would happen in a smaller place with a smaller yard. They now realize family time does not depend on where you live. Without many of the repetitive tasks required to keep up a large house and property, they have the freedom to make time for the people and things that are important in their lives.

They have benefited by not having the expenses of the large property, allowing for more discretionary income. Jeff and Margaret are a highly communicative couple with a proactive plan for retirement that they find freeing.

The Weaver family: Conversations and continuing care

David and Esther Weaver are both eighty-eight years old and live in a small apartment at a continuing care facility. They have eight children, and most live nearby. For much of their married life, they lived and farmed in northern Pennsylvania. They had been sent there by their church, which asked them to establish a mission in a rural, mountainous area. David was ordained as an unpaid pastor at the small church. About five years after their move, he severed his right arm in an accident with a corn harvester. In spite of that accident, he adapted to farming with one arm and continued to fulfill his duties as a pastor. Finances were tight; the family was close-knit.

Eventually, the children began to leave home for college or work and settled in other communities. The family connections remained strong, however, and gatherings at their parents' home occurred regularly.

A few years ago, David had several seizures. Esther and the children were concerned that the seizures posed a risk when he was on the tractor and around power equipment. Even more troubling, the hospital and doctors were an hour away. Gently, the children began planting the idea that the parents should leave the farm and move to a retirement community near to some of the children. Initially, David was not ready to give up his independence, his work on the farm, and connections he had made in the community. But he agreed to move when he realized how worried Esther was about him.

When space at the retirement home became available, David and Esther were ready to move. The adult children packed their belongings in a moving truck and transferred them to their new home. One of the children selected the furniture and pictures that were appropriate for the apartment. When the decorating was completed, the parents stepped into a dwelling filled with familiar items, and they felt like they were at home. They cherish the quilt on their bed, which was made for them by the church David pastored.

Although David and Esther say it took about a year to adjust to their new home, both are satisfied with the decision. At first David missed the open fields and felt he had lost a sense of purpose. Esther was a bit overwhelmed by being around so many people. But they began making new friends and even renewed friendships with residents they had known from childhood. They began to take advantage of the various programs on the campus. David occasionally leads Bible studies and devotions. He always enjoyed putting puzzles together and has acquired new friends who join him at his puzzle table in the common room. Esther, a retired nurse, has friends who talk with her about their medical ailments. She enjoys reading and is an avid walker. She also serves on campus committees.

The children and grandchildren visit regularly. Each child has assumed a particular role with the parents. Some take them shopping or to doctors' appointments. Some help fix up their apartment. One has power of attorney and another is medical proxy. One of the children manages the finances because the electronic banking system is confusing to the parents. They review bank statements together, and Esther continues to write the checks. The children who live in other communities call, write, and visit regularly. The siblings talk often to ensure that their parents' needs are met. They share leadership. One of the children occasionally brings her music students to the center for recitals, which David and Esther enjoy.

They feel fortunate to be where they are, and they believe the timing of the move was right. Most of all, they take comfort in knowing that their children are available to meet their needs. The daughters take their mother out to lunch on birthdays, and the sons take their father to a cabin for an annual weekend getaway. A recent highlight was an eighty-eighth birthday celebration for David. He and Esther feel blessed, and the family is happy that their parents are secure and cared for.

Ben and Sue Sprunger: Estate-planning conversations

Ben and Sue Sprunger share the following story in their own words.

As with many who raised families during the last half of the twentieth century, we shared little about our financial assets with our adult children. Perhaps our reluctance to share was a continuation of what our parents modeled for us. Knowing there were some risks, we, at age seventy, decided to break the pattern and provide full disclosure of our finances and estate plans with our children.

Our accumulated assets exceeded what we expected to achieve during our marriage. From our perspective, God has blessed us beyond our expectations. We feel we've been caretakers of his wealth, not owners. How, then, might we balance what should be given to our children with what should be given back to God, who entrusted so much to us?

Further, we have concluded that it is our responsibility to arrange our estate so that we create the least possible entanglements for our children. We didn't want to leave a mess of undocumented assets in hard-to-find places with minimal indications of what our wishes were. We concluded that failure to do careful and inclusive estate planning was not only negligent, but also a passive-aggressive response to aging and death and burdensome to our children.

Inclusive estate planning, breaking with traditions, and full disclosure can create dissonance. And since we believe that we've been given our considerable assets from God's providence, how do we give them back? Furthermore, how should we deal with our culture's expectation, not to mention our children's expectations, that assets earned are passed to descendants?

Our parents first tithed a portion of their estates; then passed their very modest estates to their children. Isn't that a birthright going back to biblical times, practiced today by most parents and encouraged by inheritance laws?

Our challenge was twofold. First, how could we minimize our children's discomfort during our full disclosure discussions? Second, could we find a win-win solution to give back to God generous amounts that were the sum of fortuitous planning, investments, and careful expenditures, while honoring our children, in keeping with their expectations? One favorable factor was that our children understood and had observed our faith priorities, tithing, economic understanding, and financial practices.

With thirty-plus years of CEO or equivalent work in higher education, foundations, and non-profits, we were aware of estate-planning options. Nevertheless, we scheduled meetings with our church denomination's foundation to explore all the options. We shared freely with them what our views were about stewardship and giving back. We then felt ready to call a family meeting to discuss our estate planning and to give full disclosure of our assets and our thinking.

Our plan was to make haste slowly. At first we mentioned to our adult children that we wanted to bring our wills up to date and wanted their participation. They demurred. Later we proposed a family meeting to discuss our estate planning. They were well aware of the various investment properties we had and favorite lake cottages in which they felt much more than a passing interest. They had no knowledge about the value of our securities and retirement portfolios.

Prior to the first meeting, we sent our children a confidential paper outlining what needed to be discussed. We provided a financial statement and a document outlining options for estate distribution. As might be expected, the children were surprised by the substance. We wanted to reduce their discomfort, so we were deliberately open and forthcoming. Our three children's responses were quite different. They continued to have varying attitudes, concerns, and differences throughout the process.

Because one of the adult children is single, we all agreed that only the three siblings would attend the first meeting with us parents. We prepared an agenda. We began with the most emotional subject first—our death and burial plans, which were already in place. We hoped that would demonstrate that we had no hesitation to talk about these and other sensitive matters.

The second item on the agenda was the distribution of heirlooms and personal and physical properties.

Over the years, we observed that distributing physical assets can be contentious and create hurts that last for years. We prepared an inventory of all items of value. We asked the children to offer options about how these things could be distributed so as to avoid painful conflicts. We discussed the pros and cons of their ideas.

The third item was where would we live and who would take care of us when we became infirmed? Since health or infirmity was not an immediate issue, we agreed to revisit this every few years.

Powers of attorney, durable powers of attorney for health care, living wills, executors, etc., were the fourth items on the agenda. After a full explanation of these, the children quickly volunteered according to their interests and abilities.

The fifth item to discuss was the distribution of assets. We shared our personal views about giving back to God while still honoring them. Not surprisingly, they expressed divergent views. Not achieving a consensus, we agreed to further exploration. However, we insisted that the options must include both honoring God's generosity as we distributed our accumulated securities, investment properties, and retirement investments, while also sharing with the children. We agreed to reserve the cottages for the children and grandchildren.

In our second family meeting a year later we focused on distributing our assets other than the cottages and personal physical property to our children and grandchildren. At this meeting, we said that we preferred to establish a charitable remainder trust. In our view, this type of trust would be a win-win solution to honor God's generosity by giving back, while also providing benefits to the children. The grandchildren would each receive a nominal cash distribution. Our children would receive four percent or greater distribution from the corpus for twenty years. After the twenty years, the corpus would become an endowed scholarship fund for students planning to enter church service positions.

Using this option, the children would receive approximately the same amount as we would give to charity. Rather than receiving their inheritance immediately, they would receive it over time. And in the end, the corpus would revert to preparing church leaders. From our perspective, this was a win-win solution. The children accepted the charitable remainder trust proposal with mixed levels of support but without objecting. We reviewed previous items from the first meeting, and then clarified and adjusted them as needed.

When we finalized all the necessary documents, we called a third meeting. We included the spouses in order to bring them into the discussion for full disclosure and clarifications. We shared copies of our wills, trusts, and the charitable remainder trust. We provided explanations and clarifications of the trust. We told them the locations of the original legal documents, along with contact information.

Each family meeting became more relaxed and informal. For the fourth meeting, we prepared no advance agenda or minutes. We gathered around the table on the deck at the cottage. We had an informal discussion, answering questions, providing clarifications, and doing some family planning not related particularly to estate matters.

There are many paths to reach satisfactory financial destinations. However, we believe it is advantageous to start early and make haste slowly when parents are in good health and children aren't pressured into choices. For us, this path seemed to provide the right balance of involving our children in decision-making, preparing for our infirmities and passing, removing obstacles in advance of death, providing full disclosure with a healthy discussion of wealth management, and ultimately honoring God by giving back what so generously came into our care and management.

Annually, we spend weeks together at the summer cottage. Family harmony and planning doesn't happen by accident. Parents must take the lead and work consistently at maintaining good relationships, resist playing one child off against another, and not only sharing beliefs and assets, but also providing an orderly process for ending our time together.

Our children seem to appreciate that we are trying to have no surprises when we leave them. While they didn't cheer about the charitable remainder trust and our benevolence, they didn't object or make disparaging remarks. All seem to be in good spirits, accepting and appreciative of their participation in the process and their parents' beliefs and values.

The Smucker family: Life-cycle conversations

The extended Smucker family has been an example of family closeness and commitment to communication over the years. Paul was seventeen years old when his father died, and about ten years later his eldest brother died of tetanus. Now the oldest of the children, Paul carried extra responsibility. The various family crises caused the family to bond more tightly. Their mother reached deep within herself to hold her eight children together. Her courage was well known throughout the community.

When Paul and his wife, Elma, were approaching their eighties, they began to plan for long-term care. They wanted to make sure that they wouldn't become a burden on their six adult children. But when they announced that they intended to move to a continuing care community, their children resisted. Instead, they proposed that the family homestead, where Paul and Elma were living, be remodeled, and that an apartment would be added on where they could live. One of the daughters, Ruth, would be offered the house at a reduced price and would assume a primary supportive role with her parents. With much gratitude, Paul and Elma gave their consent to the proposal.

In addition to working out the financial arrangement for the house, their oldest son helped his parents develop an estate plan. A large share of their assets would be given to church agencies, and the rest would be given to the children. They developed a plan in an environment of openness, and it succeeded because the siblings showed respect and grace throughout many family meetings. When differences surfaced, they would table the discussion and come back to it at the next meeting.

The outcome of their collective process benefited everyone. Over the years, a constant stream of family members came through Paul and Elma's home. Ruth was comfortable in her role as the eyes and ears for her siblings and was a source of security for her parents. Four years later, Paul was diagnosed with a brain tumor. He spent five weeks in the hospital after surgery and then returned home. During that time the extended family—including aunts and uncles—increased the support they gave to Paul, Elma, and Ruth. "Porching" became a tradition as family members gathered regularly on Sunday evenings to sing, pray, and comfort each other.

While Paul was recuperating from brain surgery, he read with interest about a buffalo roundup that was scheduled in Idaho. His four sons insisted that they all fly out together to see it. He was concerned about missing his doctor's appointments and perhaps not being able to take his medications properly. His sons assured him that the trip was more important than a doctor's appointment. The experience turned out to be very meaningful for all of them.

Soon after the trip, the tumor returned. The family decided together that they would decline any life-extending treatment. Paul was cared for and surrounded by his children and siblings at home. When his medical needs became greater, he moved into a nearby nursing care center, where he spent his last twelve weeks.

In the midst of the nursing staff and hospice workers, the entire family—all thirty-six of them—continued to gather by his side. They filled the halls of the center with song. One by one, each family member assured Paul that they were releasing him from this life and expressed their gratitude for all he meant to them over the years. Before he took his last breath, he raised his head as if to acknowledge them and then died. The legacy of family closeness continues.

The Weaver-Housers: Conversations about living and dying

Rod and Mary Lou have spent many years living in a beautiful one hundred twenty-seven-year-old brick farmhouse built on land that was granted to ancestors by the son of William Penn. This historic property is located on the rolling hills of southern Lancaster County, near some of the best orchards in the country. Behind the barn is a small cottage that Rod and Mary Lou have offered as a center for persons seeking spiritual retreat. The entire property suggests quiet reflection and a recognition of the sacred.

Mary Lou's ninety-one-year-old mother, Iona, became an extra special part of the family's life during the last year of her life. For nineteen years, Iona had been living in a retirement center more than an hour's drive away. The family received word that she was diagnosed with ovarian cancer. They knew that if she stayed there it would be difficult to visit frequently, especially as she neared death.

Mary Lou and many of her eight siblings had gathered earlier to plan for moving her mother to the Houser home, where there was an apartment available. At first Iona wasn't sure that the move was necessary, but she accepted their invitation. Before she came, there was painting to be done and a few changes to be made to the bathroom. Rod and Mary Lou's family helped with the work and was excited about having Grandma close by.

After Iona moved in, Rod served as her primary cook, providing her three nutritious meals every day. Mary Lou helped her mother with the day-to-day care, as well as enjoying serendipitous, sometimes long and meaningful discussions about her fears, spiritual questions, and other important things that they had not talked about before. Other siblings covered her financial and medical needs, as well as giving respite care to Mary Lou and Rod. Hospice workers provided some services, and a young woman from their church would sit with Iona when needed.

At first it was hard for Iona to leave her friends at the retirement center. It was even more difficult for her to give up control of her life, finances, and medications as her body weakened. She wanted to know about her physical condition and asked for updates from her health care providers. Iona even checked the bills and found a mistake in a medication charge.

The year that the family shared together was a sacred one. Not only did Iona have the pleasure of daily contacts with Mary Lou and Rod, the kittens and gardens, she also enjoyed the frequent visits of her other adult children and grandchildren. One of her grandsons hugged her closely and said, "Grandma, do you have any idea how much we love having you here?" Never to be caught speechless, she looked askance at him and warned, "If I get all mixed up and crazy at the end, will you remember to tell people who I was?"

Iona had a steady flow of visitors; some even had to wait for their turn to be with her. The house became a gathering place for her friends and extended family. Included in this parade of visitors were many of her seventy nieces and nephews.

Perhaps the most precious time occurred at the end of the day when Mary Lou and her mother spent time together. They would talk about the surprises, the inspirations, and touching moments of that day. The role reversal for Mary Lou—to provide care for her mother—was not always easy for either of them, especially as more decisions had to be made.

Mary Lou kept a journal and created an art series called *Afterglow* that reflected the experiences of the dying process that year. Earlier she had made an art piece called "Motherline" that included photographs of four generations, from her grandmother to her daughter. After Iona's death, Mary Lou's eight-year-old granddaughter, wearing a shawl when arriving for the vigil, hugged her mother and Mary Lou, wrapping them tightly with the shawl. Perhaps it was a way to symbolize the union that would continue even after her great-grandmother was gone.

Iona died on January 12, 2010, exactly one year after arriving at her new home. Immediately following her death, Mary Lou and her sisters prepared Iona's body and held a twenty-four-hour vigil, which allowed them and others to spend some precious moments with her. At Iona's request, her body was donated for medical research under the auspices of Human Gifts Registry.

A Benediction

To seniors: As you face your final life stage, do it with courage and with a spirit of expectation. Discover new ideas and purpose. Strengthen your relationships, especially with your spouse and family. Know that some of the best discoveries, and the most meaningful ones, can happen when you are no longer distracted by careers, attaining, and obtaining. Now is a time to reflect and to genuflect. Humility can be a life-expanding virtue.

Turn to your caregivers with grace and gratitude. Thank them as often as you can. Invite your adult children into your life as partners. You want them to be with you to the end. You need them and they need you—as partners.

To adult children: Set aside your doubts about whether you are entitled to become a partner with your parents. Just as you needed them when you were young, they need you now, whether they admit that or not. In the midst of your busyness, make time for them. It is an investment in their future—and yours. Most likely there are some younger eyes and ears observing what is happening between you and their grandparents. Just as our faith is carried from generation to generation, so is our legacy. Choose your legacy thoughtfully.

Questions

1. Are there any common themes in these stories?

2. What can we learn from them?

3. What is your family story about these subjects?

4. How do you think others will experience your legacy?

Endnotes

Chapter 1

1. Home Instead Senior Care, "Conversation Starters on Sensitive Senior Issues," http://www.todaysseniorresouce.com/closeup. asp?cid=89&pid=116&offset=0

2. Jeff Love, "Approaching 65: A Survey," http://www. aarp.org/ personal-growth/transitions/info-12-2010/approaching-65.html

3. Barry Rand, "New Realities of Aging," *AARP Magazine*, 12, 2010, 34.

4. Grayson R. Vincent and Victoria A. Velkoft, "The Next Four Decades," US Census Bureau, May 2010, http://www.census. gov/prod/2010pubs/p25-1138.pdf

5. Alzheimer's Association, "Alzheimer's Disease Facts and Figures," *Alzheimer's Disease*, 2 Vol. 7.

6. Institute for the Ages, http://www.institutefortheages.org

Chapter 3

1. "Social Security," http://en.wikipedia.org/wiki/Social_Security_ (United_States)

2. Guiding Lights Caregivers, 2011, http://www.guidinglightsnc. org/caregiving-statistics.php

3. Gail Sheehy, *Passages in Caregiving* (New York: HarperCollins, 2011), 51.

Chapter 4

1. Sheehy, *Passages in Caregiving*, 12, 37.

2. Ibid., 49.

Chapter 5

1. Joe Mont, "Retiring in the Red," *Newsweek*, January 10, 2011, 10.

2. Federal Trade Commission, "Fraud Against Seniors," http://www.ftc.gov/os/2000/08/agingtestimony.htm

3. Home Instead Senior Care, "The 40-70 Rule," 2010, 13.

4. Lani Luciano, "The Right Price for Care," *AARP Magazine*, November 16, 2010, 12.

5. Ibid.

6. Ibid.

7. Karen Jones, *Death for Beginners* (Fresno, CA: Quill Driver Books, 2010), 93.

Chapter 6

1. Walter Brueggemann, *The Land: Place as Gift, Promise, and Challenge in Biblical Faith* (Minneapolis: Fortress Press, 2002), 4.

2. www.cohousing.org/what_is_cohousing

3. ShalomVillages@netlinx.net

4. Stoeckel, Kimberly J. The Role of Home Environments in Residential Adjustment, Decision Making in Later Life. Doctor of Philosophy Dissertation, University of Massachusetts, Boston, 12/2011, p 6-7.

5. Eric Tyson, "Frequently Made Retirement & Estate Planning Mistakes," http://www.erictyson.com/articles/20100201

6. JanetB, Ehow Contributor, "The Average Length of Stay in a Skilled Nursing Facility," http://www.ehow.com/facts_7254573_average-stay-skilled-nursing-facility.html

Chapter 7

1. Jane E Brody, "Tackling Care as Chronic Ailments Pile Up," *New York Times*, Feb 21, 2011, http://www.nytimes.com/2011/02/22/health/22brody.html

2. Robert Fogel, "Forecasting the Cost of U.S. Health Care," *The American*, September 2009, 79.

3. United Business Media, "New Survey Shows Seniors Struggle Under Weight of Multiple Medication Use," April 2011, http://www.prnewswire.com/news-releases/new-survey-shows-seniors-stuggle–under-the-weight-of-multiple-medication-use-80246652.html

4. Joseph Coupal, "Walk and Keep Your Memory Strong," http://springarborliving.com/_blog/SpringArbor_LivingBlog/post/Walk_and_Keep_Your_Memory_Strong/

5. Sarah Beasley, "Obese Die Up to 10 Years Early," *The Guardian*, March 18, 2009, http://www.guardian.co.uk/society/2009/mar/18/health-nhs-obesity-smoking

6. Center for Disease Control & Prevention, "Falls Among Older Adults; An Overview," http://www.cdc.gov/homeand recreationalsafety/falls/adultfalls.html

7. Steve Wallace, "Age Dictates Peak in Accident Rates," http://www.driving.ca/dictates+peaks+accident+rates/2473693/story.html

8. NIH Senior Health, "Hearing Loss and Older Adults," http://www.nidcd.nih.gov./health/hearing/pages/older.aspx

9. Paula Span, "Where the Oldest Die Now," http:// newoldage.blogs.nytimes.com/2012/04/18/where-the-oldest-die-now/

Chapter 8

[1] Alzheimers Foundation of America, "About Alzheimers," http://www.alzfdn.org/AboutAltzheimers/statistics.html

[2] National Funeral Directors Association, 2010, http://www.nfda.org/about-funeral-service-/trends-and-statistics.html

[3] Sheryl Kay, Health Science Communication, 2011.

[4] Thomas Long, *Accompany Them with Singing*, 2010.

Readings and Sources

Akst, Daniel. *We Have Met the Enemy: Self-Control in an Age Of Excess*. New York: Penguin Press, 2011.

Baines, Barry K. *Ethical Wills: Putting Your Values on Paper*. Cambridge, MA: Da Capo Press, 2001.

Bent, Robert Freeman, *Forgiving your Parents*. New York: Grand Central Publishing, 1990.

Brubaker, Shirley Yoder. *Reinventing Aging*. Scottdale, PA: Herald Press, 2003.

Brueggemann, Walter. *The Land: Place as Gift, Promise, and Challenge in Biblical Faith*, 2nd ed. Minneapolis: Fortress Press, 2002.

Casarett, David J. *Last Acts: Discovering Possibility and Opportunity at the End of Life*. New York: Simon & Schuster, 2010.

Chittister, Joan. *The Gift of Years: Growing Older Gracefully*. Katonah, New York: Bluebridge, 2008.

Connidis, Ingrid. *Family Ties and Aging.* Los Angeles: SAGE Publications, Inc., 2009.

Delehanty, Hugh, and Elinor Ginzler. *Caring for Your Parents: The Complete Family Guide.* New York: Sterling Publishing, 2008.

Gibbs, Donna. *When I'm 64: The New Retirement.* Sydney: NewSouth Publishing, 2009.

Gillon, Steven. *Boomer Nation: The Largest and Richest Generation Ever, and How It Changed America.* New York: Free Press, 2004.

Jones, Karen. *Death for Beginners: Your No-Nonsense, Money-Saving Guide to Planning for the Inevitable.* Fresno, CA: Quill Driver Books, 2010.

Long, Thomas G. *Accompany Them with Singing: The Christian Funeral.* Louisville, KY: Westminster John Knox Press, 2009.

Longacre, Doris Janzen. *Living More With Less, 30th Anniversary Edition.* Scottdale, PA: Herald Press, 2010.

Miller, Glen E. *Empowering the Patient: How to Reduce the Cost of Healthcare and Improve Its Quality.* Indianapolis, IN: Dog Ear Publishing, 2009.

Schwartz, Barry. *The Paradox of Choice: Why More Is Less.* New York: Harper Perennial, 2005.

Sheehy, Gail. *Passages in Caregiving: Turning Chaos into Confidence.* New York: HarperCollins Publishers, 2011.

Spence, Linda. *Legacy: A Step-by-Step Guide to Writing Personal History.* Athens, OH: Swallow Press, 1997.

Terman, Stanley A. *Peaceful Transitions: Plan Now, Die Later—Ironclad Strategy.* Carlsbad, CA: Life Transitions Publications, 2011.

Wiebe, Katie Funk. *Prayers of an Omega: Facing the Transitions of Aging.* Scottdale, PA: Herald Press, 1994.

_____. *Life After 50: A Positive Look at Aging in the Faith Community.* Newton, KS: Faith and Life Press, 1993.

_____. *Good Times With Old Times, How to Write Your Memoirs.* Scottdale, PA: Herald Press. 1979.

For Reference

American Association of Retired Persons
www.aarp.org

Audient: An Alliance for Accessible Hearing Care
www.audientalliance.org

CaregiverStress.com
www.caregiverstress.com

Center for Strategic and International Studies
www.csis.org

Elder Law Associates of Pennsylvania
www.elderlawpa.com

Green Burial Council
www.greenburialcouncil.org

Home Instead Senior Care
www.homeinstead.com

Institute for the Ages
www.institutefortheages.org (Eric Dishman video)

LeadingAge PA
www.panpha.org

Legacy Center
www.thelegacycenter.com

MennoMedia
www.mennomedia.org

National Hospice and Palliative Care Organization
www.nhpco.org

National Institutes of Health
www.nih.gov

SCOPE, Sarasota, Florida
www.scopexcel.org

Village to Village
www.vtvnetwork.org

United States Census Bureau
www.census.gov

United States Department of Health and Human Services
www.hhs.gov

Exhibits A-H

Make as many copies of these forms as your family needs. Or go to GoodBooks.com/NecessaryConversations to download printable versions of the forms.

Needs Assessments for Caregivers

Introduction		
Tasks	**Coordinator**	**Provider**
Monitor bill paying		
Review expenses and income		
Balance checkbook		
Review investments and savings		
Review wills		
Review estate planning		

Housing		
Tasks	**Coordinator**	**Provider**
Yard and house maintenance		
Housecleaning		
Assess safety hazards		
Plan for long-term housing		

Health		
Tasks	**Coordinator**	**Provider**
Monitor health changes, nutrition		
Schedule doctor appointments		
Accompany to doctor visits		

Needs Assessments for Caregivers

Health		
Tasks	**Coordinator**	**Provider**
Monitor medications		
Maintain medical file		

Daily Activities		
Tasks	**Coordinator**	**Provider**
Encourage appropriate social activities		
Provide for transportation needs		
Assess driving skills		
Arrange for personal care services		
Monitor meals and eating habits		
Monitor shopping needs		
Coordinate visitors		

End-of-Life Planning		
Tasks	**Coordinator**	**Provider**
Review Advance Directive, Living Will, and POLST		
Encourage funeral planning		
Make sure will is correct		
Determine need for and funding of long-term care		

We suggest that adult children be given copies of this information and told where the original official documents are kept for each parent.

- Names, addresses, phone numbers of family members, including siblings
- Birth and marriage certificates, passports
- Names and contact information of agents of power of attorney and health care proxy
- List of medications currently being taken; list of any allergies (see Exhibit F)
- Health care providers, including doctors and hospital information
- Copy of Medicare or Medicaid card
- Do not resuscitate (DNR) order (see Exhibit E)
- Advance directives (living will, POLST; see Exhibit E)
- Anatomical gift/organ donation card
- Funeral plans

We suggest that parents inform their power of attorney agent(s) and their executor(s) about the secure locations where the following materials can be found.

- Social security number for each parent
- Insurance policies (see Exhibit C)
- Financial information (see Exhibit C)
- Financial statement (see Exhibit D)
- Official financial papers and documents (CDs, stock and bond certificates, annuities paperwork, loans, titles, deeds)
- Computer passwords for all accounts
- Will and testament for each parent

- List of possessions and distribution of them
- Location of the names and account numbers for each of the following, so each can be notified upon the death of the parent directly involved:
  - checking account(s)
  - saving account(s)
  - retirement account
  - annuity(ies)
  - CD(s)
  - mutual funds
  - stocks and bonds
  - life insurance policy(ies)
  - health insurance policy(ies)
  - subscriptions and memberships
  - extended family and friends

Exhibit C
Financial Information

We urge all families to seek advice from their parents' accountant, lawyer, and/or financial advisor about the extent of the information you should share below.

This list is to help you get started and is not exhaustive.

Date: _____

Name of Parent: _____

Address: _____

Phone #: _____

Social security #: _____

Bank lock box location: _____

Bank lock box #: _____

Bank lock box key location: _____

Contents: _____

Lawyer: _____

    Address: _____

    Phone #: _____

Accountant: _____

    Address: _____

    Phone #: _____

Financial advisor: _____

    Address: _____

    Phone #: _____

Exhibit C
Financial Information

Insurance

Life: _____

    Address: _____

    Phone #: _____

    Acct # and value ($): _____

    Contact info: _____

Home & Fire: _____

    Address: _____

    Phone #: _____

    Acct #: _____

    Contact info: _____

Health: _____

    Address: _____

    Phone #: _____

    Acct #: _____

Auto: _____

    Address: _____

    Phone #: _____

    Acct #: _____

Financial Institutions

Banks/credit unions: _____

    Address: _____

    Phone #: _____

    Checking/savings acct #: _____

Exhibit C
Financial Information

Investments

Stocks and Bonds: _____

    Address: _____

    Phone #: _____

    Acct #: _____

Mutual Funds: _____

    Address: _____

    Phone #: _____

    Acct #: _____

Annuities/CDs: _____

    Address: _____

    Phone #: _____

    Acct #: _____

Properties: _____

    Address: _____

    Contact Information: _____

    Acct #: _____

Partnerships: _____

    Address: _____

    Phone #: _____

    Acct #: _____

Exhibit C
Financial Information

Retirement accounts: _____

    Address: _____

    Phone #: _____

    Acct #: _____

Credit Cards: _____

    Phone #: _____

    Acct #: _____

Loans to

Institution or Person: _____

    Address: _____

    Phone #: _____

    Acct #: _____

Loans from

Institution or Person: _____

    Address: _____

    Phone #: _____

    Acct #: _____

Financial Statement

Date: _____

Names: _____

Birth dates: _____

Social security numbers: _____

Addresses: _____

Phone numbers: _____

Assets

Stocks and Bonds: _____

    $ Value: _____

Mutual funds: _____

    $ Value: _____

Partnerships: _____

    $ Value: _____

CDs: _____

    $ Value: _____

Annuities: _____

    $ Value: _____

Retirement accounts: _____

    $ Value: _____

Financial Statement

Checking accounts: _____

   $ Value: _____

Savings accounts: _____

   $ Value: _____

Non-Cash Assets

Properties: _____

   Addresses: _____

   Appraised $ value: _____

Possessions: _____

Life insurance: _____

   Address: _____

   Phone #: _____

   $ value: _____

Liabilities

Loan Amounts: _____

   From: _____

   Interest charged: _____

   Length of term: _____

Net Worth: _____

Medical File

Name: _____

Address: _____

Phone numbers: _____

Contact Person: _____

    Address: _____

    Phone #: _____

Health proxy: _____

    Address: _____

    Phone #: _____

Date: _____

    Blood pressure: _____

    Cholesterol: _____

    Weight: _____

Dates of past illnesses: _____

Dates of hospitalizations: _____

Dates of surgeries: _____

Date: _____

    Present medical condition: _____

    Symptoms and diagnosis: _____

Health Care Providers and Hospitals

Names: _____

Addresses: _____

Phone numbers: _____

Pass codes to electronic medical record file maintained by

primary physician/medical practice: _____

Location of copies of Advanced Directive, POLST, and

other legal health care documents: _____

Prescription Medications

Medication	Dosage	Frequency

Non-Prescription Medications and Supplements

_____

_____

_____

_____

_____

_____

_____

_____

Allergies

_____

_____

_____

_____

_____

_____

_____

Parent

I am entrusting you to periodically review my driving safety with me. I will accept your observations without being defensive or blaming other drivers. I will respect your advice to restrict my driving. When the time comes when I can no longer drive, I will give you my keys and permission to sell my vehicle.

Please be gentle with me if I find it difficult to lose this part of my independence.

This is my wish, and I give you permission to make the necessary decisions. Thank you for protecting me. I love you.

Signature: _____ Date: _____

Adult Child

I am humbled that you are entrusting me with this responsibility. I love and respect you for preparing with me for the time when it is no long safe for you to drive. I pledge to be gentle with you as I alert you about my concerns.

My hope is that when the time comes for you to no longer drive, it will be a mutual decision. If I need to make that decision alone, I will do so only to protect you and others.

Please be assured that my siblings and I will be available to provide transportation or make other arrangements to enable you to remain independent. I am honored and relieved that you have given me this privilege.

Signature: _____ Date: _____

Indicators of Unsafe Driving

- Easily distracted while driving
- Hitting curbs
- Having trouble merging into traffic
- Poor judgment when making left turns and at intersections
- Failing to follow traffic signs and signals
- Near crashes
- Causing dents and scrapes
- Reduced vision/relies on passenger for help
- Responding more slowly to unexpected situations
- Getting lost frequently
- Having a hard time turning around

Adapted from AARP.com

Funeral-Planning Instructions

Funeral home to be contacted: _____

Cemetery: _____

My wishes for remains:

❏ Cremated

❏ Organ donor

❏ Body to science

❏ Traditional burial

I would like services held in:

❏ Church: _____

❏ Funeral Home: _____

❏ Other: _____

I request the following person(s) to participate in the service:

❏ Pastor: _____

❏ Relatives: _____

❏ Friends: _____

Scriptures, hymns, poems that are especially meaningful to me :

❏ Scriptures: _____

❏ Hymns: _____

❏ Special music: _____

❏ Poems or readings: _____

Funeral-Planning Instructions

Suggestions for Pallbearers (usually six):

1: _____

2: _____

3: _____

4: _____

5: _____

6: _____

My clothing preference: _____

Memorial contributions: _____

Other special instructions: _____

Signature: _____ Date: _____

Adapted from AMC, Akron PA

Detailed worksheet available at:
deathforbeginners.com

About the Authors

Gerald W. Kaufman was in private practice as a therapist for 34 years. He served as a consultant to nursing homes for 15 years. His Masters in Social Work is from Indiana University.

L. Marlene Kaufman was a therapist in private practice for 24 years. Her Masters in Social Work is from Temple University.

Both Gerald and Marlene have dealt extensively with family issues in their practices, including aging and end of life.

The Kaufmans have co-authored two previous books: *Monday Marriage, Celebrating the Ordinary*; and *Freedom Fences, How to set limits that free you to enjoy your marriage and family*, written with their two daughters.

The Kaufmans have four children and eleven grandchildren.